Blessings in the Book

Demystifying the Prophetic Text
to Uncover the Blessings
—— in the ——
Book of Revelation

MARY L. PAGE, MAABS, MPA, BSBM

WESTBOW
PRESS®
A DIVISION OF THOMAS NELSON
& ZONDERVAN

WestBow Press books may be ordered through booksellers or by contacting:

WestBow Press
A Division of Thomas Nelson & Zondervan
1663 Liberty Drive
Bloomington, IN 47403
www.westbowpress.com
1 (866) 928-1240

Because of the dynamic nature of the Internet, any web addresses or links contained in this book may have changed since publication and may no longer be valid. The views expressed in this work are solely those of the author and do not necessarily reflect the views of the publisher, and the publisher hereby disclaims any responsibility for them.

This book is a work of non-fiction. Unless otherwise noted, the author and the publisher make no explicit guarantees as to the accuracy of the information contained in this book and in some cases, names of people and places have been altered to protect their privacy.

Any people depicted in stock imagery provided by Getty Images are models, and such images are being used for illustrative purposes only. Certain stock imagery © Getty Images.

Scripture taken from the King James Version of the Bible.

ISBN: 978-1-9736-2757-9 (sc)
ISBN: 978-1-9736-2756-2 (e)

Library of Congress Control Number: 2018905484

Print information available on the last page.

WestBow Press rev. date: 05/16/2018

Dedication

I dedicate this second edition of *Blessings in the Book: A Study Guide for the Book of Revelation* to all my fellow teachers, facilitators, and students of the Good News of Jesus Christ as found in the book of Revelation.

As you peruse and study this enhanced volume, may your heart be stirred to feast on the Word and share it with renewed passion and exuberance. We know that the Second Coming of our Lord is nearer than when we first believed. Therefore, let us be about our Father's business as we strive to enhance the kingdom of God, telling a dying world that Jesus is indeed coming back again just as He said He would.

Contents

𝒫reface

The mandate to teachers of the Word is to declare the everlasting, indisputable, unchangeable truth of scripture and do so with anointing, power, and clarity. The reality of our Lord's Second Coming excites the spirits and stirs the hearts of believers the world over. Christians are filled with eager anticipation as they look forward to that blessed hope, to the time when our Lord will reign forever. Jesus is coming back, and we are convinced it won't be long.

"We are living in the last days." Most of us have heard that statement ever since we first accepted the Lord as Savior and became aware of His Second Coming. This amazing truth resounded in the hearts and minds of the disciples and believers of the early church as well. They were curious and concerned about knowing the signs of His coming and of the end of the world.

Jesus did not rebuke or berate them for inquiring about this important topic. Rather, He gave them detailed instructions, cautionary words of wisdom, and some of the most specific information ever given about the Tribulation, His Second Coming, and what they could expect in the last days (Matt. 24:3ff; John 14:1–3).

This desire to know also permeated the congregations of new believers as represented throughout the New Testament. The apostle Paul said that he "would not have them to be ignorant" concerning the things of the end times (1 Thess. 4:13). God wants His people to know and be acutely aware of the signs of the times. He does not want us to be caught off guard and taken by surprise like a thief in the night (1 Thess. 5:2; 2 Peter 3:10). But this is not to say we should stray into the folly of trying to establish dates and attempting to learn things God has not chosen to reveal (Matt. 24:36; Mark 13:32).

During John's island experience, God used him to take this quest for answers to a new level. He utilized powerful and descriptive apocalyptic imagery and phenomenal, prophetic events as he toured the heavens with his personal angelic guides.

The apostles Peter and Paul and others spoke and wrote about His Second Coming; but in the book of Revelation, the apostle John takes us there not only in words but also in vivid, living color as given by God Himself. The message went from God to Jesus and then to the angel, to John, and to us, the church (Rev. 1:1), but it lost nothing in transition. Rather, the Word gained a spiritual momentum that remains and inspires believers to this day.

The challenges the church faces in the twenty-first century are the same as those faced by the first-century church—to remain vigilant, sober, and on fire for the Lord. Unlike the churches at Ephesus and Laodicea, we must be found loving Him as we did when we first met Him lest we be like those described by the apostle Peter who mocked the believers and the Word of God asking rhetorically, "Where is the promise of His coming? … For since the fathers fell asleep all things continue as they were from the beginning of creation" (2 Peter 3:3). That is to say, "We've heard this before. We're living in the last days, but He hasn't come yet. Further, the 'date-setters' have all been wrong, so why should we believe He's coming back at all?"

Rest assured, my friend. Be not deceived. The Bible is right. God is not a man who lies; neither is He the Son of Man who should repent (Num. 23:19). He's coming back just as He said. He will be coming with the fervent expectation that His bride will be ready and waiting with eager anticipation with clean and white garments washed in the precious blood of the Lamb.

The Lord wants us to see in advance how He will take revenge on His enemies. He wants us to see in advance how He will defeat Satan and his angels in a resounding victory. He wants us to take courage and hope to the end knowing that He will show Himself strong and mighty, the King of kings and Lord of lords.

So hold on and let your imagination soar as we take an extraordinary visual journey through Revelation. "Behold, the Lord comes with tens of thousands of His saints" (Jude 14). "Surely I come quickly, amen." "Even so, come Lord Jesus" (Rev. 22:20). Maranatha!

$\mathcal{A}$cknowledgments

And He gave some apostles; and some prophets, and some evangelists; and some pastors and teachers: for the perfecting of the saints and the work of the ministry and the edifying of the body of Christ.
—Ephesians 4:11–12 (KJV)

I extend a very special thank-you to my personal family of proofreaders through whom this second work was inspired. To my brother/father, the late Rev. Dr. Johnie Carlisle Jr., one of the most brilliant yet humble men I've ever known. I am thankful for your kind, professional, and loving support. Your words and our quiet times together were a constant source of encouragement for me. I miss you terribly, yet I must say, rest easy sir and I'll see you in the morning!

To my daughter, Dr. Michaelle H. Knight, you know me so very well and have a wonderful way of calming my spirit and helping me see different perspectives on the issues of life. Thank you for being a phenomenal daughter and an objective consultant. You have been trying to tell me what to do for years, and this time, you nailed it! Peace and prosperity to you in your every endeavor. I did much of what I have accomplished in life to inspire you and your siblings to do great exploits in the name of our Lord. Your inspiration has brought me full circle. Thanks!

To my daughter, Peggy Page Robinson, if there is one person who was more excited about this project than I was, it was you. You kept all my study notes since that time and shared them with your friends. Who does that? Thank you for believing in me and being the first person to go online to purchase my first book. You were a one-person marketing team. May all the blessings of the book of Revelation be yours!

A pastor, a shepherd of the flock of God, is a unique and special assignment in the work of the kingdom. To my firstborn son, dearest friend, and trusted leader Pastor Michael H. Page Sr., what an incredible man of God you are! You have never wavered in your commitment to your God, church, family, or me. Thank you for being the man God is calling for in these last days. He has equipped you for every assigned task, and I appreciate your support from the depths of my heart and soul. You are wise beyond your years, and I'm blessed to sit under your leadership. You're proud of me? No, son. It's the other way around. I could not be more proud of you and all God is doing in your life. Shalom!

A very special thank-you to my friend and "African sister from another mother", Dr. Joy Karanick Roach, Trumpet of Hope Ministries International. What a joy it was to share those precious hours of one-on-one teaching and studying God's Word with you. Thank you for your inspiration and encouragement!

It's Almost Midnight! In the Day That You Hear my Voice, Harden Not Your Heart!
—Hebrews 3:7–8, 15 (KJV)

New Seasons Ministries Inc., a Division of Henry Page Ministries Inc., presents

Blessings in the Book
Introduction to Eschatology

Mary L. Page, MAABS, MPA, BSBM

Got a question about the end times? Do you wonder if the church is really going through the Great Tribulation? What happens after death? Will we really live again for eternity? What about the babies and the children? Will Satan really be unleashed to rule this world one day? Is hell real, or is it a myth? Is the Rapture the same as the Second Coming? Join us for class and let's explore what the Word has to say.

More about the Author

Evangelist Page has served Liberty Temple Worship Center in San Diego (formerly Greater St. Paul COGIC) since 1961. Following the death of her husband in 2007, she has continued to serve under the anointed leadership of her son and daughter-in-law, Pastors Michael and Christina Page.

Along with her husband, the late Bishop Henry Page, Evangelist Page helped establish Henry Page Ministries Inc., a ministry team that has been a blessing to ministries all over the United States, Canada, and Europe. They established a primary school, planted churches, and drilled deep, fresh water wells in West Africa. To date, they have eighteen wells that supply clean, fresh drinking water to more than 90,000 children and their families. She plans to continue the work should the Lord lead because the need is great and much work remains to be done.

Mary became a diligent teacher and ongoing student of eschatology in 1984; she studied under the tutelage of some of the greatest teachers and professors of the Word of God. She has conducted "End-Times Revelation Revivals: An Introduction to Eschatology" at churches all around the United States including California, Washington, Idaho, and Missouri. Her class "Blessings in the Book" is a refreshing, inspirational, and informative tour through the book of Revelation.

In 2016 Mary was honored to teach the end-times series in Gboko, Nigeria. More than 400 people attended, and 200 copies of *Blessings in the Book, first edition* were donated to pastors from the city and the bush country.

For seven years, Evangelist Page served as dean of the School of Ministry and Licensing for Women for Southern California Second Ecclesiastical Jurisdiction. She created and designed curriculum, conducted numerous classes, workshops, and seminars for missionaries, leaders and lay members alike. She maintains a very active ministry schedule speaking and teaching at a variety of events for churches and other community organizations around the world.

Evangelist Page is a 2015 graduate of Moody Bible Institute and Theological Seminary in Chicago where she earned a master of arts in applied biblical studies. She also earned a master's degree in public administration from the University of San Francisco and a bachelor of science degree in business management from the University of Redlands. She worked for twenty years as a manager for Pacific Bell/AT&T and twenty years in health care administration at Rady Children's Hospital in San Diego.

In 2011, Evangelist Page launched her own ministry: New Seasons Ministries Inc., a division of Henry Page Ministries Inc. The ministry focuses on education, encouragement, and hope for the people of God as they navigate the changing seasons of their lives.

Mary's personal family and her Liberty Temple Worship Center San Diego family are critical components of her support system. She is seeking a fresh anointing and clear direction to do His will in this new season of her life.

Introduction to Instructors and Facilitators

Greetings, fellow pastors, instructors, facilitators, and teachers of the Word of God! Blessings to you, and peace through our Lord and Savior, Jesus Christ. What a privilege it is to have been chosen to teach and declare the Word of God and make plain the eternal truths of scripture to those who seek to know Him on a deeper and more personal level.

Your task is to lead learners through the book of Study Guides and walk them through the various sections of the material causing the Word to come alive in their hearts. Your objective is to help them increase their knowledge and understanding of the Book of Revelation. Your primary goal is to help demystify the text so they can find their place in the book and receive the blessings it contains. Once you begin to look for them, you will find them everywhere.

Simplified Study Guides

Through the use of simplified Study Guides, Revelation has been broken down into four bite-sized pieces making it easier for the student to navigate all twenty-two chapters and their topics. Various worksheets throughout the book will help students grasp the essence of the general subject matter and more importantly understand to whom it applies.

Renewed Interest—Passion Reignited

Recently, there has been widespread, renewed interest in the subject of eschatology. People are talking and reading the Bible searching for clues and asking questions about the doctrine of the last things. As the global community seems to spin hopelessly out of control, people are thirsting for a word of comfort and reassurance as we move steadily into the end times.

Many are desperate for answers that meet them right where they are emotionally, naturally, and spiritually. Even longtime, devout Christians are looking for fresh hope as they wait patiently for the promised Second Coming of Jesus Christ. Some are seeking reassurance that they will indeed see their deceased loved ones again. They simply want to know exactly where they stand as blood-washed, born-again believers in relation to the Rapture, the Tribulation, the Millennium, and eternity.

Instructors, this is your time and opportunity as teachers to positively affect the lives of your students for eternity. God has unveiled the scriptures to His people, but many of them have not yet realized that. You can be the catalyst through whom God continues to unveil His plans for eternity.

The Benefits of Blessings in the Book

Blessings in the Book: A Study Guide for the Book of Revelation is an excellent resource that can help facilitate the study of this timely and relevant portion of God's Word. This Study Guide could have been subtitled *Revelation for the Rest of Us.* Its purpose is to assist readers reveal truths previously hidden from them due to fear, lack of knowledge, or misunderstanding.

It is designed to educate and inspire while giving students a firm, basic understanding of scripture and providing a framework that will enable them to "give everyone an answer for a reason of the hope" in them (1 Peter 3:15). This Study Guide is especially designed to teach the truth of the second coming of Jesus Christ in a clear and simple manner in a way that everyday individuals can understand.

Your Mission

As a teacher, your primary goal is to facilitate learning to make it possible for the students to have light bulb moments and times of refreshing that bring them joy and peace as they eagerly anticipate the Second Coming. What sets this book apart from others is the demystification factor.

Mystique vs. Meaning

One of the most common reasons people give for not reading Revelation is that its symbolic language and prophetic nature is often difficult to comprehend. That lack of knowledge leads to fear of reading the book, but failure to read it leads to a lack of knowledge and more fear. A continued lack of understanding and fear and the downward cycle perpetuates itself.

Those who are not research scholars tend to get lost in the symbolic verbiage and miss the meaning of the passage. The arguments and debates of learned scholars have raged for centuries, and they will continue to do so. But in the meantime, many valuable hours can be spent trying to decode every symbol utilized in the text when often the meaning of the symbol is not necessarily the message the Word desires to convey.

This Study Guide seeks to take advantage of the meaning in the language of the text and follow Revelation as it is laid out. While it is necessary to acknowledge that the book is not written in complete chronological order that is not a valid reason to disregard its benefits. There is a case to be made for reading the scriptural text as it is written literally whenever possible. Study it the way it was given to the apostle John and build from there.

The Common Touch

I want this book to reach laypeople who simply want to understand the veracity and reliability of the Bible as it is. The Study Guide seeks to reach those who just want to know that Jesus really is coming back and that there is hope for a new tomorrow. No debate, no hassle—just the facts.

Jesus reached out to the Scribes, Pharisees, Rabbis, and scholars as well as the doctors and lawyers of His day. Most of them denounced Him. Despite this persistent rejection, He was concerned about them and their understanding of the kingdom of heaven. He never lost touch with common people— farmers, fishermen, publicans, tax collectors, sinners, the lame, halt, blind, mute—all who believed in Him were welcomed into His grace and love. He took time with them and created a way of teaching so common people could understand His message. He called that method parables. God promised a "blessing to those who read, hear and keep the sayings of this book" (Rev. 1:3).

The Lord did not say we had to fully interpret the text or completely comprehend every facet of the prophecy or the symbol used to describe it, but He did promise a blessing to those who would read or hear it. This is not to say that God does not want us to seek understanding and systematically study the Word; He does. We just shouldn't get sidetracked with what is versus what is not essential to salvation and to the certainty of His return

Read on—Explanations Are on the Way

The instructor/facilitator should note that in many instances, if the reader will just read on, Revelation will frequently explain itself. Remind the students they are already familiar with this style of narrative and storytelling. I call it the *Genesis Factor or Breaking News: Details at Eleven* (Mary L. Page, 2013).

News announcers are quite skilled at piquing our interest by saying, "Traffic blocked on the ABC freeway due to a major injury accident; details at eleven." We're interested, but we have to stay up until 11:00pm to get all the details—how many injuries and so on.

Note Revelation 1:13–16, for example; we see the use of symbols: "One like the Son of Man" is walking among the "seven golden candlesticks and holding the Seven Stars in His right hand." He introduces the seven golden candlesticks, the angels, the seven stars, and a sharp, two-edged sword coming out of His mouth. But if we continue reading, the symbols are decoded for us in verse 20.

The four horsemen of Revelation are introduced in chapter 6, but the full extent of their characters, purpose and the damage they will cause is revealed in subsequent chapters. This is a classic example of what I call "Breaking news! Details at eleven."

You've Seen This Writing Style Before

The writers of the scriptural text employed a similar style throughout the Bible. It is not unique to Revelation. We first see this technique illustrated in Genesis 1. God created everything, and the writer bullet-points all seven days of creation in the first chapter, the breaking-news announcement. He created man on day six in verse 27, gave the command to be fruitful and multiply, and imparted dominion. But it's not until chapter 2 that He shared additional (details at 11:00pm) about the creation of man, specifically his name, what he was made of, how he became a "living soul" through God's breath, where he lived, the instructions he received regarding the trees, and so on. It is not until chapter 3, verse 20, after the Fall that we learn the woman's name.

Matthew 13:1–8 gives us the parable of the sower and the seed in this style. The subject of the parable is outlined in the first eight verses. A Q&A session follows in which the disciples are enlightened as to why Jesus chose to teach this way. Jesus then discusses some other things with them, but the parable is not explained until verse 18.

Using this approach to Bible study allows the instructor to settle the students, ease their fears, and remind them of what they already know.

Concluding Thoughts

If you are excited about the Word, you will share it with that same enthusiasm. If you believe it, your students will know it. They will feel it as your spirits connect through faith. They will sense it as you guide them through the myriad of passages that point the way to the certain return of the Lord and a confident knowing about the will of God for His people during the last days.

Blessed is he that reads, and they that hear the words of this prophecy, and keep those things which are written therein: for the time is at hand.

—Revelation 1:3 (KJV)

$\mathcal{B}$lessings in the Book of Revelation? What Blessings?

Revelation is a fascinating book. Of all the things that have been said about it, one rarely if ever hears that it contains blessings to those who read it or hear it. It is filled with uncommon and unparalleled prophecies, symbolic language, and metaphors that can leave some frustrated, others afraid, and still others confused.

The fact that the book was not written in complete chronological order is bothersome to some people and further alienates students from the good news in its pages. Despite that, Revelation is replete with wonderful blessings, good news, and promises God made to His children. Once you begin to understand the outline and learn to whom the book is speaking, you will be blessed—guaranteed.

I believe Satan tries to keep the people of God from reading Revelation and discovering its blessings of truth. Unlike any other, this book details the end of the devil's reign of terror. It declares victory for every believer dead or alive. It proclaims the final doom of our soul's enemy.

Satan does not want us to know he will be publicly humiliated, bound, defeated, and cast into the pit of hell and specifically to the lake that burns with fire and brimstone. Most people know we will win in the end, but that's not all; we will also see the enemy of Christ going down in a permanent and resounding defeat. Revelation tells us step by step how He will do it.

Listen to this! (King James would say, "Behold!"). Allow me to share one of the most exciting blessings ever from Revelation—you absolutely have to know this. What if you received a call from an attorney informing you that an outrageously wealthy relative had died and left you something in his will? You remembered him telling you that you were his favorite and that he loved you. The attorney said the will would be read the next day at 9:00 a.m. I'm sure you would be there with the proverbial bells on around 8:00 a.m. waiting with bated breath for the office to open. No heavy traffic or wild horses would keep you away.

It's that level of excitement and anticipation and more that our Lord wants us to have about His Word. Revelation is the last will and testament of Jesus Christ, the unveiling of His plan for the end of the age and beyond. We are the beneficiaries of all He owns, so He wants us to know the plan, receive it in our hearts, and look forward to its fulfillment. Imagine how tragic it would be if you didn't go to the reading of your rich relative's will because you were too afraid. That's what it's like when believers allow fear to stop them from reading Jesus's last will and testament.

Regardless of why we do not read this portion of the Word of God, the result is the same. If we don't read it or hear it read to us, we won't know it, and that means we can't live in the freedom it offers. We end up living beneath our privilege in fear or ignorance. Jesus is saying, "Come; let me show you how I'll deal with those who denied Me, the Christ, the Messiah, the Son of the Living

God. Let me show you how I'll bring all things under complete subjection of the Father." Jesus is telling us to read the scriptures and see how He will rule and reign forever.

This Study Guide will help you navigate those passages actively looking for the will of God and the blessings in Revelation. Let me bullet-point some of these blessings.

- Revelation is not a stand-alone book tacked on to the other sixty-five as an afterthought. It is the same God-breathed, God-inspired, unchanging Word of almighty God as was spoken of in Genesis, in the books of the law, the prophets, the gospels, and the epistles. It completes the full canon of scripture and meets all the criteria that were applied to all the other texts.

  For example, the book had to have been written by an eyewitness to the works of Christ, and it had to have been written within the first one hundred years after His death and resurrection. The apostle John and the writings revealed to him certainly meet those criteria.

- Revelation is not the only book that deals with end-times prophecies and God's final plan for the ages. If you are afraid to read Revelation, you must also be afraid to read the other epistles or even the gospels of Matthew or John. You must never read 1 Thessalonians, 1 Corinthians, 1 or 2 Peter, or Jude. You must never read the Old Testament books of Isaiah, Zechariah, or Daniel. I could go on, but I think you get the point. Revelation is the culmination of all that was spoken of and promised in the other books of the Bible.

- Revelation is the movie version of the Bible in that the other books of the Bible tell us about the last things, but Revelation shows it to us and fills in the details. If you let your imagination go and follow the apostle as he takes you on a panoramic view of the last days, the church, the Tribulation, the Millennium and beyond, you will be in for a fantastic treat.

  Sometimes, a really good book comes out and someone makes a movie of it. For a variety of reasons, people will prefer one genre to another. One person may have authored the book, the screenplay might have been written by a different writer, and the movie created by yet another artistic professional. In some cases, funding is a problem and the movie doesn't quite match the book. In the case of our God, however, the author, producer, and the financier are the same.

  Sometimes, the cost of taking the production to a different location in another country is the issue, but not in this case. The earth and everything in it is the Lord's (Ps. 24). With its vivid pictures and imagery, Revelation is an exact replica of the book God wrote. Let's go to the spiritual movie theater.

- Revelation is the only book in the Bible that promises a blessing, in the first chapter, for those who "read and those who hear" the words of this prophecy. Notice that God did not say we had to fully comprehend each chapter and verse; He did not say we had to decode every symbol and peer ever so deeply into the mind of God. We can read it or hear it, believe it, and be blessed.

- It is a blessing that if you just continue reading, many of the passages will explain themselves. See the following scriptures for example: Revelation 1:20, 4:5, 7:4, 7:13–14, 13:15–18, and 17:7–8. The symbols have a timeless application that allows different nations and peoples in all times to learn the same truths without the interference or distraction of cultural or linguistic challenges.

- There's victory all throughout the book. Even when it looks as if Satan will win, he never does. Read and watch God as He gains each victory!
- The saints overcome the world; we will inherit all things and reign with Him forever and ever.
- We get a glimpse of our rewards in heaven.
- We visit the throne room of the Most High.
- We see God sitting on the throne in ultimate splendor.
- God details how He takes revenge on all His enemies and those who denied His name. He told us to let Him take care of our enemies saying, "Vengeance is mine, I will repay, says the Lord." (Romans 12:19)
- Satan is defeated for all time in Revelation.
- Sorrow, sickness, pain, death, and hell are defeated forever.
- There are amazing songs of praise and worship throughout the book. Look for them!
- The model for worship is not found in any other New Testament book. All heaven and everything in it bows before and worships the God of the universe, the Holy One of Israel. What a blessing!
- The Lord wins major war victories. He acts out 2 Chronicles 20 right before our eyes. The Lord told Jehoshaphat that he would have no need to fight in the battle because the battle was not his but the Lord's. The saints will be at the battle, but we will not need to fight. We will see God defeating His enemies with only the brightness of His glory. That's a phenomenal blessing!
- Revelation shows us the unbelievable—peace in Jerusalem and the whole world. Now that's good news!
- The promise of eternal life is manifested in this incredible book, and that's the best news ever!

Revelation is filled with blessings of all types, and our Lord wants us to know them and praise Him for them. God shows Himself to be everything the scriptures say He is. He's the King of Kings, the Lord of Lords, the Almighty. All power in heaven and on earth is in His hands and under His unquestioned authority. You must read these blessings for yourself!

Instructor Notes: Course Syllabus

The instructor should review the course syllabus with the class. I designed it to provide an outline and flexible scheduling options for pastors, teachers, Bible study leaders, facilitators, or anyone tasked with determining the length of the series as deemed appropriate for a group.

For groups that meet once weekly, the series generally works best when spread over six to eight weeks. For some groups, four or five chapters per session may be too much depending on how much detail and discussion the instructor desires to go into. For others, four or five chapters may be just right depending on homework and out-of-class reading as assigned.

The Revelation Four Point Outline is ideal for class sessions that need to be shorter and more succinct. Using this tool to cover the four points as outlined, is simplified and straightforward. Once the class understands the four basic parts and to whom the prophecy is directed, it becomes easier to delve into the sections and discuss them as a whole or by chapter and verse.

For some churches, or bible study groups the class can also be taught in a full-week format with five two-hour classes nightly and a full or half-day session on Saturday. In any case, the intent is to show flexibility and offer a solid overview of the book of Revelation. The students will know exactly what they are going to study and obtain a good idea of the material to be covered.

Notes Q&A
Food for Thought

_____

_____

_____

_____

_____

_____

_____

_____

_____

_____

_____

_____

_____

_____

_____

_____

_____

_____

_____

_____

_____

_____

_____

Course Syllabus

Blessings in the Book, the Study Guide is an introductory course in eschatology that provides a comprehensive look at the book of Revelation. The course summarizes all twenty-two chapters in manageable, easy-to-understand segments. Students will learn the principles, prophecy, purpose, and promises of the blessings in the book.

The class will focus on how Revelation fits into the entire canon of scripture and where believers stand in relation to the prophecies of the book. The sessions are designed to demystify the Word and thereby eliminate the fear of reading this incredible book. It serves to inspire students to renew their vision, passion, and hope for the soon return of our Lord.

Revelation Is Not a Stand-Alone Book

Revelation is the culmination of what began in Genesis at the creation of the world. It was prophesied by the prophets, promised by Jesus, and taught by the apostles in the gospels and epistles. Revelation is the manifestation of the Messiah coming the first time as our Suffering Savior and coming back a second time as King and Judge. All of heaven and earth look forward to Jesus's coming in power and glory. You must read the details in this marvelous book!

God does not want us to be ignorant (1 Thess. 4:13–18). He wants us to know His plan and that He is faithful to His Word (Rev. 1:1–2). He said, "Vengeance is mine, I will repay" (Deut. 32:35; Rom. 12:19). Hell was created for the devil and his angels, not for His bride, the church. Read the last will and testament of Jesus Christ to learn what He is preserving for us, His beneficiaries, as well as for His enemies.

There are four major views on the Rapture and the Tribulation: Pre-Tribulation, that is that the church will be raptured before the Tribulation; Mid-Tribulation, that the church will be raptured in the middle of the Tribulation, and Post-Tribulation, the belief that the church will be raptured after the Tribulation. A-Tribulationists believe the church will not be raptured at all or some version of the above beliefs.

Eschatological scholars have debated and will debate this subject until Jesus comes. Don't fret about the opinions and speculations of others or what they believe. You can trust the promises of God and stand on His Word and reputation. The scripture is clear regarding the promises of God to His bride, the church. God is not angry with her; she has been purchased and made pure by the shedding of the blood of His Son, Jesus Christ. Our sins were blotted out at Calvary. Through belief and repentance, our punishment has been covered by the finished work of Christ on the cross.

*P*roposed Course Outline

Week 1—Chapters 1–5

Introduction and overview of Revelation, the seven churches of Asia Minor, the Rapture, and a glimpse into the throne room of heaven.

Week 2—Chapters 6–10

The Tribulation—first three and a half years; the 144,000 evangelize; the seven seals and the seven trumpets; the beginning of the worst seven years in the history of the world. Five months of torment, no death; 200 million–man army. The little book, bittersweet.

Week 3—Chapters 11–14

The Great Tribulation, two witnesses, new world leader reveals true character, chaos erupts worldwide, the Sun-Clothed Woman, protection for Israel, Satan marks his people, fate is sealed. Unholy trinity in full swing, 144,000 in heaven with the Lamb.

Week 4—Chapters 15–19

The seven last plagues (bowls/vials), Euphrates dried up, judgment of the Great Whore, false church, Babylon is fallen, Battle of Armageddon ends the Tribulation, vile fowl called to the Supper of the Great God, armies of Satan are defeated, Jesus comes in glory! Marriage Supper of the Lamb.

Week 5—Chapters 20–22

Christ victorious at the Battle of Armageddon, Beast and False Prophet cast alive into lake of fire, Satan bound for 1,000 years, Millennium, peace, and long life. Satan loosed, joint heirs reigning with Christ, Great White Throne Judgment, books opened, New Jerusalem, heaven on earth, Jesus reigns, eternity, Maranatha!

Week 6 and/or 7

Wrap-up and review as needed. Stay rapture ready—shalom!

Instructor Notes: End-Times Prophecy Pre-Test

The pre-test is actually not a test at all at least not in the usual sense of the word. But it's a lot of fun to watch the students' faces when they think it is. Students are instructed to take the pre-test using true or false responses and feel free to guess at any answers they do not know.

The test will not be graded by anyone other than the students themselves. It will become a training resource to be referenced as needed. The students' faces will relax. The class can review the correct answers and scriptures as a group, and the students will be encouraged to look up the scriptures as homework.

The instructor may also choose to allow time during class to take the test and score it at that time. The pre-test serves at least three purposes.

1. Its primary function is to offer students an effective way to assess their knowledge and discover in a user-friendly format where they can enhance their knowledge.

2. It is a ready resource when students have questions or desires to explore a particular subject or theme; they can refer to the questions and answers and find exactly what they are looking for.

3. The pre-test is a great icebreaker. None of us knows everything about the book of Revelation, so the pre-test provides a fun yet educational opportunity to level the playing field. As the class goes through the questions and answers, everyone can learn something new in a nonthreatening environment.

If the subject comes up, caution the students that although the answer sheet is in the back of the book, looking up the answers first produces a lesser degree of learning. It is best if they follow the syllabus as outlined—taking the pre-test first and checking the answers individually or as a group. They can search the scriptures to see if their responses are supported in the Word. Either way, the information is passed on and the students will have a great resource for future study.

End-Times Prophecy Pre-Test

Answer True or False

Test your knowledge. How much do you already know about the end times? Compare your growth and knowledge before and after you take this class.

This worksheet is for your information and study only. It will not be graded or corrected except by you. We will review it at the beginning of class and again at the end to compare your knowledge growth level. Write "true" or "false" for each question.

_____1. The word *rapture* occurs frequently and unmistakably in scripture.

_____2. Believers as well as unbelievers will have to go through the Tribulation.

_____3. God's purpose in allowing believers to go through the Tribulation will be to purify the church.

_____4. One purpose for the Rapture of the church is to take the saints to heaven where they will receive their reward.

_____5. The Holy Spirit will be removed from the earth at the Rapture.

_____6. The real purpose of the Great Tribulation is to deal with all unbelievers, punish them for their sins, and deal with God's chosen people, the Jewish nation of Israel.

_____7. During the Tribulation, no one will be saved.

_____8. It is advisable to wait until the Great Tribulation to get saved so God will know how strong you are.

_____9. There is evidence in the world today of the Mark of the Beast.

_____10. The Battle of Armageddon is not mentioned in the Bible.

_____11. The Battle of Armageddon is the final battle of all time.

_____12. The Rapture and the Second Coming are one and the same.

_____13. The belief that Jesus will come back to earth and set up an earthly kingdom is completely symbolic and a figure of speech.

_____14. King David will actually rule over a portion of the Lord's millennial kingdom.

_____15. The earth will be populated during the Millennium, and these people will go up to New Jerusalem to worship the Lord.

_____16. A host of angels will bind Satan for 1,000 years.

_____17. New Jerusalem will be the capital city of the millennial kingdom.

_____18. After the 1,000 years have been completed, no one will ever serve Satan again.

_____19. Hell and the lake of fire are the same place.

_____20. One day, the saints will gather around the great white throne for judgment of our sins.

_____21. New Jerusalem will come down from heaven to earth.

_____22. We will be bored to tears in heaven because we will just sing and pray all day.

_____23. Just like in church, there will be no eating or drinking in the New City.

_____24. Does it really matter if you are Pre-Tribulation, Mid-Trib, or Post-Trib?

_____25. The saints will be invited to the Supper of the Great God.

_____26. The saints should be fearful of Revelation because it contains the details of scary things about the end of the world.

_____27. Although the church-age saints may not be among the 144,000, we are definitely in that number that no man can number.

_____28. The church will be at the Battle of Armageddon.

29. Are you saved? Yes _____ No _____

30. Are you sure? Yes _____ No _____

Instructor Notes: A Reason for Hope— Seven Reasons for a Pre-Wrath Rapture

Blessings in the book are written and taught from a pre-wrath perspective, that is, it promotes the belief that the Rapture will take place prior to the Tribulation period and that God will take the church to heaven before He unleashes His wrath on the earth. It seeks to make clear that the Lord's church has been saved, delivered, set free, and purified by the shed blood of Jesus Christ and that alone.

It also seeks to make clear that the church is the bride of Christ and has through faith and prayer been made worthy to escape the wrath of God. This view is supported by various scriptures and provides the comfort that Paul spoke at length about it with the Thessalonian church (1 Thess. 5:9 KJV).

A review of the background literature reveals that the new believers in Thessalonica had been receiving some troublesome news from those Paul described as "false teachers". He likened them to Satan and that "wicked" one who was to "be revealed" (2 Thess. 2:1–6). These teachers were promoting false doctrines including the idea that those who had died in the Lord (the deceased, saved loved ones) had missed the Rapture and therefore would not be able to go to heaven. Worse yet, they taught that if there was such a thing as the resurrection of the dead, these new converts had missed it as well. Needless to say, they were distraught and sought words of comfort from the pastor.

The apostle Paul went to great lengths to rebuke this error and refute this false doctrine. He encouraged the believers to understand that God had not forgotten them or their deceased loved ones. He told them they would be awakened from the dead with the "trump of God and the voice of the archangel" and that the dead in Christ would actually rise first! Then, those believers who were alive and remained (potentially you and I) would be caught up together with the deceased believers to meet the Lord in the air. He closed with the tender reassurance that they were to "comfort one another with these words."

If Christian believers have to look forward to struggling through seven years of tribulation, such as the world has never known, running from the Antichrist, risking life and limb, and experiencing torture and death at every turn, wherein does the comfort lie? We are confident in this; that if we have accepted Christ as our Savior, we will *not* be left behind! We will all be changed in a moment, in the twinkling of an eye and rise to meet the Lord in the air; and "so shall we ever be with the Lord" (1 Thess. 4:13–17; 1 Cor. 15:51–52).

A Reason for Hope: Seven Reasons a Pre-Wrath Rapture

1. **The main reason for hope is God's reputation**, His historical performance. We can stand on His promises. God promised Abraham never to destroy the righteous with the wicked (Abraham: Sodom and Gomorrah, Genesis 18:22; Noah: the flood, Genesis 7:1). God always preserved the righteous remnant. You can trust Him to be faithful to His Word, because He cannot lie (Num. 23:19).

2. **Hell was created for the devil and his angels** (Matt. 25:41; 2 Thess. 1:5–10; Isa. 5:14). The church is the bride of Christ. Jesus promised us a place of rest and restoration with Him in His Father's house (John 14:1–4; Eph. 5:27–29; Rev. 19:7–8, 21:19). Vengeance and tribulation are promised to them who know *not* God and obey *not* the gospel of Jesus Christ (1 Thess. 5:9–11; Luke 21:34–36).

3. **We are the righteousness of God** (2 Cor. 5:21). When we repented of our sins and were saved by the blood of Jesus, our sins were washed away. We were and are guilty, but Jesus took our place on the cross and made us sons and daughters of the King. Therefore, when God looks at us, He sees the righteousness of Christ shining through us. No wonder we love Him!

4. **The Tribulation is a time of Jacob's trouble.** It is a time when God will deal with the Jews as a nation and judge all sin. Because our sins were paid for on Calvary, we are no longer enemies of the cross. This judgment is called the Day of the Lord and the Day of His Wrath, a horrific time of judgment designed to bring Israel to her knees in repentance (1 Thess. 5:1; Zech. 14:1; Matt. 24:21; Rev. 6:16–17). According to the prophecy of Daniel, God has unfinished work with the nation of Israel. There is an unfulfilled "week" of trials and tribulation promised to them for their unbelief. The Tribulation is that week. It was never promised to the "Church".

5. **God has not appointed us unto wrath**. When we receive Christ as our personal Lord and Savior, the Father no longer sees us as unwashed, unrepentant sinners. He sees Jesus, the perfect sacrifice, the One with whom God is well pleased. As a result of this phenomenal transfer of the penalty for sin, He is not angry with His bride. He does not desire to punish us by unleashing His wrath upon us. He longs to bring us to His house, where we will spend eternity with Him. Jesus said, "If it were not so I would have told you." "If I go, I will come again and receive you unto myself that where I am, there you may be also" (John 14:2–3 KJV).

6. **The Second Coming is in two stages.** At the Rapture (Greek *harpaizo*), Jesus comes *for* His saints. It will be secret, like a thief in the night, and quicker than the blink of an eye (1 Cor. 15:50). At the Second Coming, He comes *with* His saints, and every eye will see Him. He will come with great glory and royal splendor. All the hosts of heaven, the church included, and the resurrected saints will come with Him (Jude 14:24).

7. **The Pre-Wrath Rapture of the church**, the bride of Christ, is the only acceptable viewpoint that brings real comfort and hope to the people of God. It is the only widely accepted view that aligns with scripture to give blessed assurance of deliverance from God's wrath and eternal hope. It provides comfort for those who mourn their deceased, saved loved ones as taught in Paul's epistle to the church at Thessalonica and to all those who love His appearing. Our previous appointment with wrath has been cancelled. Praise God for the blood!

ℛevelation at a Glance: A Four-Point Outline

The following, *Revelation at a Glance: A Four-Point Outline* is a marvelous study tool. It is my personal, all-time favorite, study aid because it divides a potentially complicated subject matter into four simplified groupings.

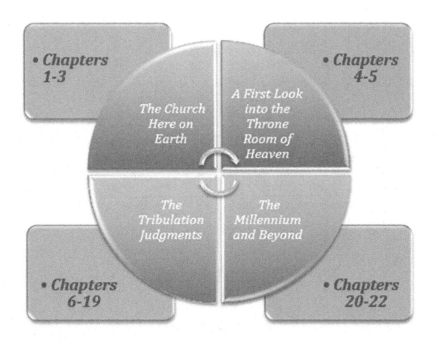

1. Chapters 1–3—the church here on earth
2. Chapters 4–5—a first look into the throne room of heaven
3. Chapters 6–19—the Tribulation judgments
4. Chapters 20–22—the Millennium and beyond

While it may be difficult for some students to interpret multiple prophetic utterances, symbolic images, times, peoples, and places, it is not difficult to view the book in four smaller and more-manageable sections.

This approach removes a great deal of fear, frustration, and feelings of overwhelming confusion. It allows students to develop confidence and believe that they can understand from a basic foundational perspective what the book is all about and to whom it is generally speaking. The mystique is decreased, and real learning can begin to take place. Once that happens, students can take the next step of "intentional reading" and "active searching", looking for the blessings in the book (Mary L. Page, 2016).

What a blessing it is to know that God really does keep His Word even during the most difficult time in the history of humankind. He shows us how He will take revenge on all the enemies of Christ. He systematically and methodically wreaks havoc on earth destroying His once-magnificent creation with mathematical precision. He defeats Satan publicly and shows His power over everything and everyone who opposes and rejects Him.

An added blessing of Revelation is that God does not simply say what He's going to do; He also shows His people in advance and in detail *how* He will do it. Let's take this journey together and see what God has in store. Our God reigns!

The Book of Revelation at a Glance: A Four-Point Outline

To expedite our understanding of what could be a very complicated and lengthy study, let us look at Revelation in as clear and simple a manner as possible. The Book has been divided into four straightforward sections.

1. Chapters 1–3 deal with the church on earth. The letters are from God to the seven churches, which include us, the modern-day church. God gives acknowledgments, warnings, and promises to His church for the end times. The book is God's plan, His last will and testament He gave to Jesus Christ, who gave it to the angel, who gave it to the apostle John, who wrote it and sent it to real churches in Asia Minor, modern-day Turkey, but they are applicable and relevant to all churches throughout the church age.

2. Chapters 4–5 open with a first look into heaven's throne room. We see something phenomenal! There is an open door, a throne; someone is sitting on the throne with a face shining and glistening like a diamond and a ruby. He has no ethnic identity that can be described, no color by which we can identify Him, yet we know Him. He is in each of us. He is the great I AM in the fullness of His glory.

   We see a rainbow, but not like those on earth. It's emerald green and encircles the throne. Twenty-four elders, representatives of the Old and New Testament saints, are seated before the throne. They are dressed in white robes and have crowns. They join the heavenly hosts in giving praise and worship to God as they lay their crowns at the feet of the One on the throne.

   The One sitting on the throne is holding a scroll in His right hand. It is sealed on the inside and the outside with seven seals. The scroll contains the Will of God for the last days. It must be opened and implemented.

   God searched the heavens, the earth and beneath the earth. No one could be found who was worthy to open the seals, or even to look upon the book. Unless the seals are opened the Will of God cannot be done in the last days. Behold! The Lion of the Tribe of Judah has prevailed! Praise and worship break forth, and all of heaven joins in.

3. Chapters 6–19 cover the Tribulation Period in vivid, living color and precise detail. God shares His plans to wreak havoc on the devil and his angels and all those who are the enemies of Christ. Jesus exacts vengeance on all who refused to honor Him as Lord, as God in the flesh, the Holy One of Israel.

   God will complete His plan for Israel, and she will do what He appointed her to do from the beginning. He uses symbols and colorful language, and we see a side of Jesus we have never seen before. He shows Himself mighty, the King of kings and Lord of lords.

   Satan declares war against God and does everything in his power to overcome God's people on earth, but he is defeated in a resounding victory.

   As we journey through the Tribulation period, remind students of this wonderful truth: we, the bride of Christ, the church for whom He died, His beloved, will sit in heavenly places with our Lord. He is not angry with us. We are not the targets of His wrath but of the phenomenal love and the many blessings He has in store for us.

4. Chapters 20–22 tell us about the end of time as we know it and the beginning of eternity. We will see God bringing into focus the reality of the Millennium and the binding and releasing of Satan while the Beast and the False Prophet are cast alive into the lake of fire and brimstone. We will see the bride, the Lamb's wife, for she has "made herself ready." New Jerusalem reveals herself as she comes down from God out of heaven in full, majestic glory.

Using this basic four-point outline, the learners are able to gain a foundational understanding of Revelation in a global sense by reading it first just as it is laid out. Studying the Word as God gave it to the apostle John can be a refreshing and nonthreatening way to begin our unforgettable journey.

Once you determine to whom the Lord is speaking and where on the timeline of eternity we find ourselves, it is less difficult to get lost in the prophetic text and the symbolic imagery. Sit back, relax, and enjoy the journey. Let the reading of the last will and testament of Jesus Christ begin.

Instructor Notes: Revelation Chapter Summary

The Revelation Chapter Summary is a great study tool designed to give readers a brief overview of what is in each chapter of Revelation. Summaries are useful for many reasons, but the chief one is that they can condense large blocks of information into structured, well-thought-out presentations.

This summary serves as a quick reference guide to all twenty-two chapters. They are listed in a few concise sentences making it easy to find the desired information based on the chapter.

Notes Q&A
Food for Thought

_____

_____

_____

_____

_____

_____

_____

_____

_____

_____

_____

_____

_____

_____

_____

_____

_____

_____

_____

The Book of Revelation Chapter Summary

Chapter 1

Introduction and identification of the divine authorship of the book; instructions to John, pronouncement of blessings on the readers, hearers and doers; the Apocalypse or the unveiling, the revealing, Alpha and Omega, the beginning and the end, the seven churches named.

Chapters 2–3

Letters to the seven churches in Asia Minor, real churches representative of all churches throughout the ages.

Chapter 4

The church is "raptured" (Greek *harpaizo*)—caught up, grasped hastily, or snatched up (Greek *episunagoge*) "complete gathering." Representatives of church and elders and possibly Old Testament saints seated around the throne worshipping the Lamb with the angels. The church is not spoken of again until the end of the book.

Chapter 5

The book of the seven seals; who is worthy? Only the Lamb of God.

Chapter 6

The seven seals opened. The four horsemen of Revelation—white horse (pseudo peace/conquering), red horse (peace taken, bloodshed, sword), black horse (famine, high prices), pale horse (death, souls under the altar crying out for vengeance). Initial introduction of the Tribulation characters—details to follow!

Chapter 7

The 144,000 are sealed by God prior to judgment falling on the earth. The Word specific as to whom these evangelists are. There are 12,000 unmarried godly men (Revelation 14:1-6) from each of the named 12 tribes of Israel. They are sealed and sent.

Chapter 8

The seventh seal is opened. Silence in heaven, the quiet before the storm; seven angels with seven trumpets.

Chapter 9

The trumpet judgments continue. The fifth angel—demonic release; torment and torture, no death for five months; Euphrates River dried up; 200 million–man army from the East.

Chapter 10

The little book, John's bittersweet experience.

Chapter 11

The two witnesses evangelize; call miracles down from heaven; slain, dead bodies lie in streets—no burial for three days. Then a miracle.

Chapter 12

The Sun-Clothed Woman, the Dragon, and the Man Child spared for a time, for times and a half time (three and a half years). According to the scripture in Daniel 9, the Jews used "time", singular, to equal one year. They used "times" plural, to equal two years, and a half time to cover the remaining 6-month period. The total is therefore 3 ½ years.

Chapter 13

The Beast out of the sea, the rise of the Antichrist, the False Prophet, miracles and wonders (deadly wound healed), the Mark of the Beast.

Chapter 14

The 144,000 in heaven with the Lamb, the Father's seal, sung a new song, three angels with messages.

Chapter 15

Seven angels with the seven last plagues; those with victory over the Beast worship the Lord God almighty.

Chapter 16

Seven angels pour out their plagues on the earth, the water, and all creatures. Some worship in the midst of it all; others curse and blaspheme the name of God. Demons, unclean spirits, gather for the Battle of Armageddon on Mount Megiddo at the Great Day of God almighty; massive hailstones fall; people blaspheme God's name.

Chapter 17

The judgment of the Great Whore—Mystery Babylon; the Mother of Harlots.

Chapter 18

The fall of Mystery Babylon—the new world system (religious and political mingle).

Chapter 19

Much worship and praise. Guests are called to the Marriage Supper of the Lamb for the bride has made herself ready. After the wedding, the King and His armies come from heaven. Another supper—the Supper of the Great God. The Beast and the False Prophet are cast alive into the lake of fire. The Second Coming of Christ.

Chapter 20

The bottomless pit, an angel, and the Dragon. The Great White Throne Judgment. Death and hell go to hell—the lake of fire. Satan bound for 1,000 years then loosed for a "little while"; tries to deceive the nations again; the battle of Gog & Magog (Russia involved?).

Chapter 21

A new heaven and a new earth; a brief description of the outside, peripheral portions of the city; the nations serve God, bring their glory to the city. The Millennium—Jesus reigns.

Chapter 22

The river of water of life, two special trees, the nations serve God; final warnings and exhortations: "And behold I come quickly and my reward is with me … Alpha and Omega, the beginning and the end, the first and the last … Surely I come quickly." Maranatha! That means, "Even so come Lord Jesus!" Amen—and it is so.

The end and the beginning.

Instructor Notes: Brief Overview
Proposed Sequence of Events

Here is something helpful for the systematic, visual learner. Each of us learns differently. Some of us need to see the scriptures laid out in charts and diagrams complete with pictures and side notes. Others of us can sit and digest that same Word just by reading it or listening to a speaker and making an occasional note. Whatever your style, this Study Guide has something to offer the typical adult learner.

The objective of this section is to provide a proposed sequence of events that is succinct and to the point. The chart is an overview and a guide. It is accurate in its content as it is stated in scripture. Revelation is not necessarily recorded in chronological order, but following the book as it is laid out is a great place to start and build your understanding from there.

Notes Q&A
Food for Thought

_____

_____

_____

_____

_____

_____

_____

_____

_____

_____

_____

_____

_____

_____

_____

_____

_____

_____

Brief Overview: Proposed Sequence of Events

1. **The Rapture of the Church**

    Also known as the Rapture of the true believers, the bride of Christ. Dead believers will be resurrected, and living believers will be caught up to meet the Lord in the air (1 Thess. 4:13–18; 1 Cor. 15:51–54; Eph. 5:22–32; Rev. 19:7–9, 21:2, 9).

2. **The Tribulation Part One—Three and a Half Years**

    After the church is raptured, chaos erupts. The Antichrist emerges and answers the entire world's question, solves its problems, and makes a treaty with Israel. Works great signs and wonders; recovers from mortal wound, brings a pseudo peace.

    Satan totally in charge; wrath of God poured out upon the world. The Antichrist sets up one-world government and religion, and 144,000 Jews saved and sealed.

    Two prophets sent out to evangelize the world, and the Tribulation begins (Rev. 13:1–5, 11–18; Dan. 9:24–27, 11:36–39; Zeph. 1:14–18; Prov. 1:24–29; 2 Thess. 2:1–12; Rev. 11:3–13, 14:1–5, 7:4–8, 7:1–4; Matt. 24:1–31; 1 Thess. 5:2–4).

3. **The Great Tribulation Part Two—Three and a Half Years (The Middle of the Week)**

    The treaty with Israel will be broken; the Abomination of Desolation, the Antichrist, shows his true colors. Jesus describes the Great Tribulation as being something that has "never been since the beginning of the world to this time, nor shall ever be" (Matt. 24:21). God avenges the rejection and death of His Son; massacre of Tribulation saints, unholy trinity; enemy in full control, the Mark of the Beast.

4. **Antichrist Overly Confident**

    The Antichrist has exalted himself; thinks he is God. Knows that Jesus is coming back and that he has only a short time left (Rev. 16:13–14, 13:4).

5. **Armageddon—The Great Battle**

    Antichrist and False Prophet cast alive into the lake of fire. Satan not cast in at that time; millions will be slain. Enemies of Christ join forces to try to stop his return. Can't be done. Blood as high as a horse's bridle; blood ran for 200 miles; Supper of the Great God/Feast of scavengers and vultures; all birds commanded to eat the flesh of men (Rev. 16:13–19, 19:19–20; Ezek. 39:1–7; 2 Thess. 2:8).

6. **Jesus Christ Returns to Earth in Glory**

    Jesus Christ came the first time (at the Rapture) for his saints. The second time, he comes with his saints. The first time was secret (like a thief in the night); the second time, "every eye shall behold him" (Rev. 19:11–16, 1:7; 2 Thess. 1:7–9; Jude 14).

7. **Judgment of Nations**

The Lord will judge the nations in existence according to the way they treated his brethren, the 144,000 Jewish evangelists. He will judge nations as individual believers will have been resurrected and raptured. Lost sinners will still be sleeping in their graves.

They will be resurrected and judged at the Great White Throne Judgment when the books are opened. When Jesus comes, He will judge the nations. The sheep (believers) will go into the millennial kingdom; here on earth, the goats (unbelievers) will be cast into the lake of fire (Rev. 19:15; 1 Cor. 6:2; Isa. 2:1–4; Matt. 25:31–46).

Let's Review

- The church has been raptured (1 Thess. 4:16–17).
- The Tribulation has become a reality. The Great Tribulation has become a reality.
- Jesus has returned to earth in glory (Rev. 1:7).
- His saints and the angels are returning with him (Jude 2; 2 Thess. 1:7–10).
- He stands on the Mount of Olives (Zech. 14:3ff). Not sure which scripture I was trying to quote here. Will check and possibly delete.
- The Antichrist and False Prophet are cast alive into the lake of fire (Rev. 19:19–20).

The armies have gathered against the Lord in battle; they are been slain, and the birds eat their flesh (Rev. 17–19).

- The Jews have looked to Jesus and owned Him as their Messiah (Phil. 2:9–11).
- Living nations have been judged; enemies of the Lord (the Beast and the False Prophet) have been cast into the lake of fire. Satan is not sent to the lake of fire then.

Are we ready for a thousand years of peace and prosperity with Jesus? Not yet. Satan must be bound first. There can be no real peace as long as Satan is loose (Rev. 20:1–3; Isa. 14:12–15).

What's Next?

- The Lord sends one angel to bind Satan and cast him into the bottomless pit, where he remains for a thousand years (Rev. 20:1–3). The earth is returned to its original, Eden-like state (Isa. 11:6–10, 65:19–25). We can enter the millennial kingdom here on earth and live a thousand years (a Sabbath day) with Jesus.
- Resurrected tribulation believers along with those who survived the tribulation are entering the millennial kingdom for 1,000 years to live, rule, and reign with Christ (Matt. 25:31–33; Rev. 20:6).
- The Great White Throne Judgment takes place. All deceased unbelievers who missed the Rapture are resurrected and must stand before God, and the books will be opened (Rev. 20:11–15). Anyone whose name is not in the book will go to the lake of fire and brimstone. None of their names will be there or they would have been resurrected 1,007 years before.

  Revelation 21–22 describes New Jerusalem and tells of a new heaven and a new earth. The New Testament believers—the church, the bride of Christ—will join the Lord for the Marriage Supper of the Lamb. Imagine being in a wedding and reception that is truly out of this world!

- Jesus reigns as King of kings and Lord of lords with His chosen people in His earthly kingdom. We assist Him in facilitating judgment on those who entered His kingdom at the start of the Millennium. People will live, have children, be judged, and be healed by the leaves on the Tree of Life that, incidentally, bears twelve kinds of fruit per year—a different fruit every month. Life will be as it was in the Garden of Eden.
- At the end of the millennial reign, Satan will be loosed for a "little season" (Rev. 20:7–10). Those born during the Millennium will never have had the opportunity to choose Christ because Satan was bound for that time. Upon being loosed from the bottomless pit, he will immediately go out to deceive the nations. Unfortunately, many will follow him. He will gather the armies of the north (Gog and Magog aka Russia; Ezek. 38:1–6ff; Rev. 20:7–10) to battle against the Lord and His people. The battle will be brief; Jesus will send fire down from heaven to devour them. Then, the devil that deceived them will be cast into the lake of fire, where the Beast and the False Prophet are to be tormented for eternity.

Jesus will reign from His heavenly kingdom. Thy Kingdom come, thy will be done, in earth as it is in heaven. Now, let eternity begin. Our Lord reigns. Maranatha! Even so come Lord Jesus, the end and the beginning.

Instructor Notes: The Seven Churches of Asia Minor

The study of the seven churches of Revelation is perhaps one of the most familiar portions of this prophetic text. Most Christians have had some degree of teaching on the subject of the churches. They are generally aware of the faults and failures of the churches as well as their areas of excellence. The placement of this study at the beginning of Revelation is strategic for us today in that we are members of the church age. It is therefore much easier to relate to, and it is a great place to start our study.

The objective of this session is to have students understand key factors about the churches including but not limited to these.

- The seven churches were real; their locations can be traced to cities in Asia Minor today.
- The apostle John wrote the letters to the churches when he was banished to the island of Patmos in the Mediterranean for preaching and teaching the gospel.. Revelation 1 tells us the letters were dictated by God to Jesus Christ, from Jesus Christ to the angel, from the angel to the apostle, and from the apostle to the churches. They have been passed down to us through the generations. They were included in the original canon of scripture and are the inspired Word of God to His people.
- The apostle John wrote Revelation for the seven churches of the first century but also to the churches of today.
- The provided worksheets will let students experience the feel of actually looking through Revelation to obtain information as well as inspiration.
- The intent is not that each response on the worksheet will mirror the instructor's responses but that the student will have a clear idea of the character, nature, and works of each of the churches.
- Reaffirm the fact that God is indeed omniscient, omnipotent, and omnipresent. He sees and knows all about us and the church congregations of all times. He was there with John on the island, He was there moving among the churches, and He's here with us today.
- Watch closely as you may see yourself or the characteristics of your church listed somewhere among the seven. As the body of believers, we have been informed and warned—our Lord is coming back for His church. "Therefore be ye also ready: for in such an hour as ye think not the Son of Man cometh" (Matt. 24:44 KJV).

Seven Churches of Asia Minor Worksheets

Instructions

Read the appropriate scripture as noted below. Complete the blanks using information from the scriptures. Your responses may vary slightly from the answer sheet at the end of the Study Guide, but that's okay. The point of the exercise is for you to discover the key character traits and spirit of each church thereby arriving at a picture of what each church was like. Do this for all seven churches. Think about how these churches may be like your church or a church you have known or heard about.

To: The Angel of the Church at Ephesus (Rev. 2:1–7) Church 1

From:

    I. The Acknowledgment (what God knows about the church):

   II. The Indictment (what God has against the church):

 III. The Requirement (what God requires the church to do):

 IV. The Ultimatum (the bottom line—what the church must do or else):

The Church's Battle against the Enemy Continues into the End Times

To: The Angel of the Church at Smyrna (Rev. 2:8–11) Church 2

From:

I.   The Acknowledgment:

II. The Prophecy:

III. The Requirement:

IV. The Ultimatum:

V.   The Blessing/Promise:

Notes on the Nicolaitans

The churches at Ephesus and Pergamum had among them those who held to the doctrine of the Nicolaitans, which God hated. The church at Ephesus was commended for hating that doctrine, but the church at Pergamum was rebuked for tolerating it.

While there is some discussion and disagreement as to exactly who was the leader or originator of that doctrine, there is no disagreement as to the evil of their doings. Nicholas, from Antioch, was a deacon in the new church, but there is no evidence that Nicholas was in any way responsible for a group of Israelites who fell into idolatry (Rev. 2:6, 15; Acts 6:5).

The issue is the Nicolaitans followed the doctrine of Balaam, a wicked OT prophet who "seduced" the people of God to eat things sacrificed to idols, to worship idols, and to fornicate. On behalf of Balak, King of Moab, Balaam tried to curse the people of God and asked God (Jehovah) to curse them. When that didn't work, he convinced Israel to turn against her God and follow the doctrine of Balaam.

The greater insult was that some in the NT church followed or tolerated this evil doctrine (Num. 22–25). It is a dangerous thing for the church to turn from God and follow idols or tolerate those who do. Israel was punished greatly for her sin. In one instance, 24,000 perished in one day because Israel joined herself to Baal of Peor and committed harlotry with the women of Moab (the descendants of Lot and his daughter).

To: The Angel of the Church at Pergamos (Pergamum; Rev. 2:12–17) Church 3

From:

    I. The Acknowledgment:

    II. The Indictment:

    III. The Requirement/Ultimatum:

    IV. The Exhortation—what the church was encouraged or admonished to do:

    V. The Blessing/Promise:

Notes Q&A
Food for Thought

_____

_____

_____

_____

_____

_____

_____

_____

_____

_____

_____

_____

_____

_____

_____

_____

To: The Angel of the Church at Thyatira (Rev. 2:18–29) Church 4

From:

I. The Acknowledgment:

II. The Prophecy:

III. The Requirement:

IV. The Ultimatum:

V. The Blessing/Promise:

Notes Q&A
Food for Thought

_____

_____

_____

_____

_____

_____

_____

_____

_____

_____

_____

_____

_____

_____

_____

_____

_____

To: The Angel of the Church at Sardis (Rev. 3:1–6) Church 5

From:

I.   The Acknowledgment/Indictment:

II. The Requirement:

III. The Ultimatum:

IV. Additional Acknowledgment:

V.   The Exhortation:

VI. The Blessing/Promise:

Notes Q&A
Food for Thought

_____

_____

_____

_____

_____

_____

_____

_____

_____

_____

_____

_____

_____

_____

_____

_____

To: The Angel of the Church at Philadelphia (Rev. 3:7–13) Church 6

From:

    I.   The Acknowledgment:

    II.   The Beholdings:

    III. More Acknowledgments:

    IV. The Indictment:

    V.   The Requirement:

    VI. The Final Exhortation:

    VII. The Blessing/Promise:

Notes Q&A
Food for Thought

_____

_____

_____

_____

_____

_____

_____

_____

_____

_____

_____

_____

_____

_____

_____

_____

_____

_____

_____

_____

To: The Angel of the Church at Laodicea (Rev. 3:14–22) Church 7

From:

I.   The Acknowledgment:

II. The Indictment:

III. The Requirement/Ultimatum:

IV. The Exhortation:

V. The Blessing/Promise:

Oh, Sing Unto the Lord a New Song!

Instructor Notes: The Revelation Hymn Book

As many students of the Word are aware, Revelation is known for many things but not generally as a source of inspiration for songs and hymns. Virtually every Christian this side of heaven is familiar with the greatest biblical songbook ever written, the book of Psalms. But rarely if ever would you hear someone rave about the beautiful songs found in Revelation. Songs in the midst of all that tribulation? Yes, they are there!

At this point in your studies, you can utilize the skill of intentional reading and active searching. With deliberate intent and careful thought, read the sacred text and think about the words to some of the most beautiful songs that offer the hope of heaven, the assurance of eternal life, and the resurrection of the dead. Think about the songs that declare the promises and blessings of the risen King. You just might be surprised and begin to see this book in a new light.

Because Revelation shows a side of Jesus we have not seen before, the songs describing and praising Him are equally indicative of a Jesus we have yet to behold. A host of songs praise and celebrate the awesomeness of the only true and living God! We hear Handel's Hallelujah chorus: "King of Kings Hallelujah, Hallelujah and Lord of Lords, Hallelujah, And He Shall Reign Forever and ever, Hallelujah, Hallelujah or Hallelujah, Salvation and Glory, Honor and Power Unto the Lord Our God. He is Great! Yes the Lord Our God is Omnipotent, Yes the Lord Our God, He is Wonderful, or We Shall Behold Him … Then Face to Face …" These and a host of other songs, including the old black spiritual "I Know I Been Changed … the Angels in Heab'n' Done Signed my Name" come directly from Revelation or were inspired by it.

All heaven is singing to, praising, and giving glory to God. How wonderful it is to realize that we, the bride of Christ, the church He died and was resurrected for, can sing along with them and honor Him with some of the most beautiful music this side of heaven. Prepare to be amazed!

Notes Q&A
Food for Thought

_____

_____

_____

_____

_____

_____

_____

_____

_____

_____

_____

_____

_____

_____

_____

_____

_____

_____

_____

_____

_____

_____

_____

_____

The Revelation Hymn Book

Some of the greatest songs and hymns of all time have their lyrics taken directly from Revelation. In the Old Testament, we have songs written by Moses, Miriam, Hannah, and others. The psalmist David and a handful of other psalmists dedicated an entire book (actually five books) to some phenomenal songs and hymns offering praise and worship to our God. These scriptures have brought hope and encouragement to the body of Christ for centuries.

However, a closer look at the New Testament reveals no book comparable to Psalms, no model of worship for the church that Christ purchased with His own blood. That is, until you get to Revelation, where we find a surprising twist. In the middle of the worst devastation known to humankind and woven throughout a book that strikes fear and trepidation in the hearts of believers all over the world, we find the words and the inspiration for some of the most beautiful songs of worship and praise ever penned. The wonderful thing we see here is that while the angelic choir and all heaven is singing and worshipping God, believers all over the world, churches, groups, and choirs, and you and I are all singing along with them.

Consider the following songs that are inspired by or found only in the book of Revelation.

1. "Hallelujah, Salvation and Glory, Honor and Power Unto the Lord Our God." He is great, yes the Lord our God is omnipotent (Rev. 19:1, 6).
2. The sky shall unfold, preparing His entrance. "We Shall Behold Him, then face to face" (Rev. 1:7, 6:15–17, 22:4).
3. "You Are Alpha and Omega, We Worship You Our Lord, You are Worthy to be Praised" (Rev. 1:8, 11; 4:11).
4. Handel's Messiah: "And He Shall Reign Forever and Ever. Hallelujah … King of Kings, Hallelujah, Hallelujah, and Lord of Lords" (Rev. 19:16, 11:15).
5. "Blessed, blessed are the dead that die in the Lord. They shall rest from all their labors and receive a just reward … I know you will be blessed, blessed if you die in the Lord" (Rev. 14:13).
6. "I know I Been Changed … You Know the Angels in Heav'n Done Signed my Name" (Rev. 20:12–15).
7. "In the Morning When I Rise, resurrection morning, great gettin' up morning, wanna see Jesus" (1 Thess. 4:13-18).
8. "Now, Behold the Lamb, the Precious Lamb of God" (Rev. 4:2, 5:5–6).
9. "Holy, Holy, Holy, Lord God almighty" (Rev. 4:8b).
10. "Worthy is the Lamb, to receive power … blessings and honor and glory" (Rev. 5:12–13).
11. "I Shall Wear a Crown … When it's all over …. I Shall Wear a Crown." (Revelation 4:4)
12. "Death could not hold you down. Seated in Majesty. You are the Risen King." (Revelation 4:2-4ff, 5)
13. "He Reigns Forever, He Reigns Forever, He Reigns Forever and Ever more."
14. "My God Reigns, Our God Reigns, Lord you Reign above Every Name."
15. "I Can Only Imagine what it will be like."

And so many others. Just read Revelation intentionally and look for them!

Instructor Notes: The Tribulation Judgments

It would be difficult to find a portion of Revelation that sparks fear, hopelessness, and confusion more than those portions that speak about the Tribulation period. Scholars, pastors, and teachers generally agree that this will be a time of unprecedented trouble and horror that has never been seen before in all of human history. They also generally agree that it will last for seven years.

Where some disagreement comes in is on the timing of the Tribulation as it relates to the Rapture and the Millennium and whether the church will be raptured prior to it, in the middle of it, at the end of it, or not at all. This Study Guide follows the mainstream interpretation of scripture that adheres to the belief that the church will be "snatched out," "hastily taken away" (Greek *harpaizo*), a "complete gathering" (Greek *episunagoge*) prior to the start of this horrible time. Scripture supports this view throughout 1 and 2 Thessalonians and other books of the sacred text.

Once the restraining power of the Holy Spirit is removed—when the church is taken away—the wicked one, Satan, will be released and the unholy trinity will be unleashed—the Antichrist (Beast), the False Prophet (Antispirit), and the devil himself, the Dragon, that old serpent, to have his way in the earthly realm (2 Thess. 2:6–9).

The argument in favor of or against the Tribulation and its timing is key to the comfort Christ promised believers—a home not made with hands but eternal in the heavens (2 Cor. 5:1). The church was promised to be taken to a mansion in the Father's house (John 14:1), and it is instructed to pray to be counted worthy to escape (Luke 21:36).

The apostle Paul admonished the new believers to "wait for His [God's] Son from heaven, whom He raised from the dead, even Jesus, which delivered us from the wrath to come" (1 Thess. 1:10). According to this passage, our deliverance from wrath is in the past tense—"*delivered* us from wrath." When Christ died for our sins on the cross, He said it was finished, it was a done deal. The moment we believed, it was already done!

"But thou, O Daniel, shut up the words, and seal the book (scroll), even to the time of the end: and knowledge shall be increased" (Dan. 12:4 KJV).

Daniel's Seventieth Week

(Daniel's Prophetic View of the Tribulation)
The Timeframe of the Tribulation according to the Prophet Daniel

The prophet Daniel had been in captivity for sixty-eight years. He was about sixteen when he was taken with his people, the Jews, to Babylon. While studying the prophecy of Jeremiah 25:11, he realized the seventy-year period was nearing an end, and he sought the Lord in prayer. Daniel was concerned and prayed about his sin, the sins of the people, the expiration of the seventy years, the restoration of Israel to the land of Palestine, and the rebuilding of Jerusalem and the Temple (Dan. 9:3).

While he was praying, the angel Gabriel appeared to him to enlighten him (Dan. 9:20–23). Gabriel told Daniel that God would fulfill his promise regarding the seventy years of captivity and said something even more important—while Israel would return to Jerusalem at the end of the seventy years of captivity, there would be a longer period before the kingdom would be restored to them—seventy weeks (Dan. 9:20–27). God gave Daniel a vision and revealed to him that the seventy weeks would be divided into three periods consisting of seven weeks, sixty-two weeks, and one week.

History notes that the Jewish people counted the weeks as years. That is, one day equaled one year so one week equaled seven years. Calculating the dates confirms that the Lord was speaking of prophetic weeks, each one representing seven years. The Jews utilized 360 days as a calendar year, not the 365 or 366 (leap year) we use today. It's important to understand this because it is the key to two critical facts.

1. This prophetic block of time refers only to the Jewish people. When He spoke to Daniel via the angel Gabriel, He clearly said that the prophecy was to "thy people" (Dan. 9:24). God had not even introduced the concept of a church, this previously unknown group of people for whom He would provide the gift of salvation through the shed blood of His own Son.

    Consequently, to assume that the Tribulation is for the blood-washed believers in Jesus Christ is not at all in keeping with the context of this prophecy. While we are the seed of Abraham by faith and adoption and heirs to the promises made to him, it would be erroneous to insert ourselves in this prophecy. Hell has indeed enlarged (Isa. 5:14) because of the wickedness of the people, but God's plan for His church is not Tribulation and hell's fire.

2. The length of the Tribulation is directly tied to the time the angel Gabriel shared with Daniel. The calculation of the weeks is important because there is no basis for attempting to make the seventieth week any different from the other sixty-nine (Dan. 9:24) Seventy weeks times seven equals 490. Here's what that means.

- From the edict in 445 BC to restore and rebuild the walls of Jerusalem to the completion of the walls would be seven weeks of years, or forty-nine years (Neh. 2:1).
- From the edict to rebuild the walls in 445 BC until the Messiah came and would be cut off would be sixty-nine weeks. That is, sixty-two weeks plus the initial seven weeks.
- Jesus rode into Jerusalem in AD 30, exactly 483 years or sixty-nine weeks after the edict. The Messiah was "cut off" or crucified sixty-two weeks after the walls were rebuilt. Note, today we refer to A.D. as "after Death". It is more accurately interpreted in its Latin translation as "In the year of our Lord". That solves the issue of the three years that Jesus ministered in human flesh.

That leaves one week unaccounted for and yet to be fulfilled. It must be the same length as the other weeks—seven years. There is no gap between the first two sets of weeks, but there is a gap between the sixty-ninth and the seventieth weeks. We are living in the space now, and the seventieth week is coming!

Daniel describes that week clearly detailing the Antichrist and the "covenant he will make with many (Israel) for one week" (seven years; Dan. 9:27). He said the Antichrist would "break the covenant in the middle of the week" or three and a half years into the agreement. He will cause the sacrifice and the oblation (i.e., burnt offerings) to cease. He will desecrate the temple and perform abominable acts of sacrilege. The Jews will be horrified that the one they thought to be their savior or messiah is not at all who he purported to be.

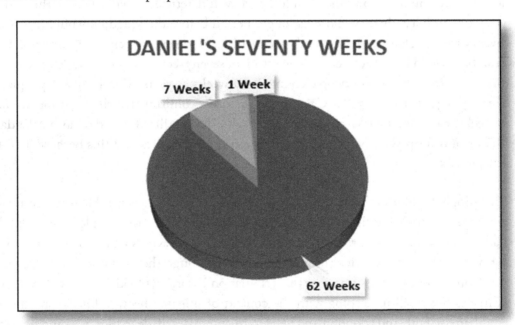

Time is running out—repent of your sin now while there's still time!

During the Tribulation, God will continue dealing with His chosen people, the Jews. They were the people He first embraced. He chose them and called them to do a work for Him. The fact that they refused to obey Him and blatantly rejected Him does not negate the reality that they were chosen to spread the gospel of Jesus Christ. That mission was not rescinded; they were not given a pass on the assignment. Unfortunately for the Jews, their mission must now be done under the most difficult of circumstances—the time of the Tribulation.

In Revelation 7, our Jewish brethren are brought on the scene, sealed with the seal of the Living God, and anointed for ministry during the worst seven years known to humankind. Jesus said in Matthew 24 that there had never been a time like the Tribulation and that there never would be. Your students must know that Jesus spoke those words in Matthew 24. If He said it would be a horrendous time, it will be horrendous.

Twelve thousand saved, dedicated, virgin Jewish males from each of the twelve tribes of Israel will evangelize the length and breadth of this world preaching the everlasting gospel of Jesus Christ just as they were called to do in the first century. Their preaching and witness will reap a spiritual harvest greater than any revival we have ever seen, and a phenomenal number will be saved. John declared in his first-century vernacular that the number he saw, "no man could number the multitude" (Rev. 7:9). Although most will have to give their lives for their faith, they will be resurrected to eternal life. Read on to see how the story ends.

Notes Q&A
Food for Thought

_____

_____

_____

_____

_____

_____

_____

_____

_____

_____

_____

_____

_____

_____

_____

_____

_____

_____

_____

_____

_____

God's Series of Tribulation Judgments

The Seven Seals, Seven Trumpets, and Seven Bowls (Rev. 6–19)

The Tribulation narrative shows a side of the Lord we have never seen before. He came the first time as a meek and humble Lamb. He was born in a stable under conditions that no person I know would submit to. He allowed his enemies to spit on Him, hit Him, and crucify Him in the most degrading manner known to humankind at that time. He hung His head and never said a word in protest. His disciples and followers were disappointed and shocked beyond belief. Yet God had promised to take revenge upon His enemies, punish the wicked, and rule in majesty. He said he would reign as King of kings and Lord of lords. But during His time on earth, the only thing written about His royal status was done in jest as they mocked him with the crown of thorns and the title King of the Jews etched on His cross.

The Second Coming will be quite different. He will come in majesty with a phenomenal display of power. Every eye will behold Him, and all earth will bow before Him. Before that happens, however, He will wreak havoc on this earth. His tone will have changed. He will no longer be humble and timid. He'll be angry, and the whole earth will experience the fullness of His wrath. Massive destruction and horror will be unleashed on the inhabitants of the world. Jesus said there has never been a time like the tribulation and there never would be again.

The following Study Guide summarizes the three sets of Tribulation judgments. All fourteen chapters of God's fury organized in three pages, one for each set, each progressively and cumulatively worse than the one before. Because the church has been made clean and whole and worthy by the blood of the Lamb, it has nothing to fear from these verses. Jump in and see in vibrant, descriptive detail what God has in store for Satan and all those who choose to follow him. Time is running out for a sinful world!

The Seven Seals Chart

God's Series of Tribulation Judgments Against the Earth: The Seven Seals (Rev. 6:1–17)	
The Seven Seals	**The first series of judgments to be unleashed on the world are called the seven seals, which are fixed on a great scroll. The scroll is progressively unrolled with the breaking of each seal.**
The First Seal	Releases the Antichrist. He begins his mission of world conquest (Dan. 8:23–25)All the world worships him (Rev. 13:4). Says "peace and safety" (1 Thess. 5:3). Persecution worldwide; false teachers and false prophets. Establishes and breaks covenant with Israel. Stops its manner of worship; desecrates temple. Israel warned to flee to the mountains (Matt. 24:15).
The Second Seal	War begins; red horse goes out. Power to take peace from the earth. Arab armies launch all-out attack against Israel (Dan. 11:40–41; Zech. 12:2–3). Soviet Union invades by land, sea, and air. Double-crosses Egypt, takes Africa too. News from the north troubles Soviet commander; Western Europe; News from East—Oriental forces (Dan. 11:44; Rev. 6:12). Soviet army returns to Israel—ultimately annihilated (Dan. 11:45; Ezek. 38–39; Joel 2:20).
The Third Seal	Global economic catastrophe, worldwide economic collapse. After war in Middle East, oil halted, and chaos sets in. Food very expensive; two measures of wheat for a day's wage (Rev. 6:5).
The Fourth Seal	One-fourth of humankind dies with the opening of the fourth seal. Pale horse named Death; power to kill (Rev. 6:7–8).
The Fifth Seal	The Massacre of the saints; horrible persecution of believers. Antichrist launches wholesale slaughter of believers (Rev. 13:5–7). Institute monetary program; implementation of 666 (the mark of the Beast). No jobs, unable to buy or sell unless swear allegiance to the Beast and take the mark.
The Sixth Seal	Nuclear war; what all nations fear becomes reality. Conventional war up to this time. Soviet Union launches first (Ezek. 39:6). Indication is nuclear exchange between Soviets, Europe, possibly US and China. The world is horrified, but the worst is yet to come.
The Seventh Seal	The seventh seal is opened, and there is a lull in judgments. God gives space for people to repent. The seventh seal releases the next series of judgments, which are more severe and increase in intensity.

The Seven Trumpets Chart

God's Series of Judgments Against the Earth: The Seven Trumpets(Rev. 8:1–13, 9:1–19)	
The Seven Trumpets	The second series of judgments to be unleashed on the world are called the seven trumpets. They are released by the seventh seal and are more severe and intense than the first set of judgments.
The First Trumpet	The first trumpet brings a burning of a third of the earth's trees, grains, and grasses, etc. This could be the result of firestorms started by numerous nuclear explosions of the sixth seal. Massive loss of vegetation, soil erosion, floods, mudslides, and air pollution. The smoke of the fire will fill the air. God is still merciful in that He leaves two-thirds of the earth untouched … for the time being.
The Second Trumpet	Great nuclear, naval battle. Convoys of merchant ships and warships destroyed. One-third of all ships and life in the sea destroyed (Rev. 8:8–9).
The Third Trumpet	One-third of the world's water is poisoned. Droughts, bitter (poison) water; many die from drinking the water (Rev. 8:10–11).
The Fourth Trumpet	A judgment against light reaching the earth. Light from the sun, moon, and stars is diminished by one-third. Both day and night will be one-third darker than usual (Rev. 8:12). Imagine the chaos and fear that is already gripping the world. Add darkness to this.
The Fifth Trumpet	Just before this judgment begins, an angel flies through the earth warningthat the worst is yet to come (Rev. 8:13). Smoke comes up from the bottomless pit; more darkness, locusts with scorpion-like power. Hurt all those without the seal of God in their foreheads. Power given to them to torment the people for five months. People will seek death but will be unable to find it.
The Sixth Trumpet	200 million–man army from the East attack (Rev. 9:12–19). Four wicked and powerful fallen angels are released to inspire the destruction of a third of all remaining humankind. Remember, one-fourth destroyed by the fourth seal; poisoning kills many more. Remaining population reduced by another third.
The Seventh Trumpet	Humanity is given one last chance to repent before the most horrible and extensive judgment of all time hits the earth. No repentance! (Rev. 9:20–21, 11:15). Apparently, all who are going to repent have done so by this time. All others have taken the mark of the Beast and are doomed forever.

*N*otes Q&A
*F*ood for Thought

_____

_____

_____

_____

_____

_____

_____

_____

_____

_____

_____

_____

_____

_____

_____

_____

_____

_____

The Seven Bowls Chart

God's Series of Judgments against the Earth: The Seven Bowls or Vials (Rev. 15:1–8, 16:1–21)	
The Seven Bowls	The third and final series of judgments to be unleashed on the world are called the seven bowls or vials. They are released by the seventh trumpet and are more severe and intense than the previous sets of judgments were.
The First Bowl	A great voice from the temple telling the seven angels to go their way and pour out the wrath of God on the earth. The first bowl brings a grievous sore, cancerous-like plague on all who have taken the mark of the Beast or worshipped his image. God will divinely protect the believers from these plagues.
The Second Bowl	The second angel pours out his judgment on the sea. This bowl judgment turns all sea water on earth to blood like the blood of a dead man. Everything in the ocean dies.
The Third Bowl	The third angel pours out his bowl on the rivers and fountains of waters, and they became blood. This angel confirms the righteousness of God's judgments because his enemies have shed the blood of the saints and the prophets and God has given them blood to drink.
The Fourth Bowl	The fourth angel pours out his vial on the sun. Power was given to him to scorch people with fire. People were scorched with great heat, and they blasphemed the name of God, but they repented not of their sins nor did they give God the glory.
The Fifth Bowl	Fifth angel pours out his vial on the seat of the Beast, and his kingdom is full of darkness. Dark clouds allow the 200 million–man army from the East to advance toward Israel.
The Sixth Bowl	Great river Euphrates dries up. This allows the 200 million–man army from the East to attack Israel. Demonic power, unclean spirits like frogs out of the mouth of the Beast, and the False Prophet causes the nations to gather for the Battle of Armageddon. It will be a suicide mission; the Lord will defeat them in a resounding victory (cf. Dan. 11:45; Ezek. 39:1–6).
The Seventh Bowl	Judgment against the air, voice from heaven—"It is done!" Thunder, lightning, greatest earthquake world has ever known. Babylon (Iraq) split into three parts, the cities of the nations fall, e.g., New York, Los Angeles, Paris, Rome, Tokyo, and London. Every island and mountain fled, huge hailstones fall; people blaspheme God.

Paradise Awaits. Eternity is calling
RSVP Required!

Instructor Notes: The Millennial Reign of Christ

And the Bridegroom tarried. Unfortunately, for some believers and nonbelievers, this tarrying of the Bridegroom has caused many to succumb to the slumber and sleep of complacency and a posture of complete apathy. Ask the class if they remember a time when just the thought of heaven, peace on earth, and eternity with the Savior would make their hearts leap in their chests.

There was a time when new converts would find themselves gazing into the heavens to see what they could see; they were daily looking for their Lord. Ask the class, "Do you remember when if you even thought that you had offended someone you would quickly apologize as you didn't want anything to hinder you from rising to meet the Lord in the air?"

Because the Bridegroom has tarried, some have stopped looking for Him. Others are living good lives but have no joy, no passion (Matt. 25). Like the Ephesian church, some don't love Him as they used to, and that hurts the Lord's heart. How would you feel if someone you loved without measure told you, "I love you, but I'm not *in love* with you"? *What in the world does that mean?* you wonder. That's the way some people treat the Lord. I love you for the goodies and gifts you give me, but I'm just not in love with you anymore. What a travesty!

The millennial reign of Christ is not a cute fairy tale; it is the gospel truth. If Jesus said it, He meant it! He did not talk just to hear His own voice. He spoke with deliberate forethought. He did not put the Word in the heart of His prophets just because He had nothing else to do. He promised that one day we would rule and reign with Him and that He would bring a new heaven and a new earth into existence. He promised that there would be a city, New Jerusalem, coming down from God out of heaven, and yes, with streets of gold and gates of pearls. What a marvelous time we have to look forward to.

He stated that the wolf and the lamb would lie down together in incomparable harmony. A little child could play in the den of a poisonous viper and experience no harm. People would live long, happy, prosperous lives as God had intended from the beginning. What manner of place is this? It is a phenomenal place of unbelievable beauty and peace. The war is over. Satan is bound, Eden is restored, and Jesus reigns!

It is imperative that you, the instructor, read some of the sacred text to the students. Remember, God promised a blessing to those who read and those who hear the prophecies of this book. Take the time to review the list of characteristics on the next page of the Study Guide and see how the class is blessed.

Encourage your students to get excited again! Renew the passion and the purpose of their lives. Fall in love with Jesus all over again. Every Word He spoke is true whether it came through the mouth of the Lord directly or through the lips and the pen of His prophets. Encourage the class to remain vigilant. Be sober and stay watchful. It won't be long.

Notes Q&A
Food for Thought

_____

_____

_____

_____

_____

_____

_____

_____

_____

_____

_____

_____

_____

_____

_____

_____

_____

_____

The Millennial Reign of Christ

> And the Lion (Wolf) and the Lamb shall lie down together.
>
> —Isaiah 11:6–9

The Millennium is an amazing time such as has never been seen since the beginning of creation. The word *millennium* comes from the Latin *mille,* meaning thousand, and *annum,* meaning year. A bullet summation of the characteristics and purpose of the Millennium is as follows.

- Christ fulfills His promise to reign with King David and the saints as King of Israel and of all the earth (Jer. 30:9; Ezek. 34:24; Hos. 3:4).
- Every knee will bow and every tongue will confess that He is Lord (Phil. 2:9–11).
- It is known by multiple names such as the kingdom of heaven, the kingdom of God, the kingdom of Christ, the age to come, a Sabbath Day, and others (Isa. 2:12, 13:6; Joel 2:1; Zech. 14:1).
- Satan will be bound, and the earth will be at complete peace (Rev. 20:1–3; Isa. 2).
- Jerusalem will be the capital city, the center of worship. It was known as Salem in Abraham's time, Shalom, peace (1 Chr. 23:25, 33:4-7; Joel 3:17).
- The Jews will worship in the millennial temple (Ezek. 43:7; Zech. 6:12–14).
- Knowledge of the glory of the Lord will fill the city (Isa. 11:9; Hab. 2:14).
- Health and long life will be restored; paradise will be restored (Isa. 35:3–6, 65:20–22).
- People will live in harmony with beasts—lions, lambs, wolves, leopards, and poisonous snakes (Isa. 11:6).
- The Millennium will be ushered in by the Battle of Armageddon as Christ defeats the armies of Satan (Rev. 19:20:1–4).
- The Millennium draws to a close with Satan being loosed for a short season, launching a final attack, the Battle of Gog and Magog, against those mortals who survived the Tribulation.
- Unrepentant sinners will be judged at the great white throne (Rev. 20:7–10).
- Hell is real, not figurative. The lake of fire that burns with fire and brimstone is real. At the beginning of the millennial reign of Christ, the Beast (Antichrist) and the False Prophet (False Holy Spirit) are cast alive into the lake of fire to be doomed forever (Rev. 19:20–21).
- Jesus spoke of hell often. Some of the best descriptions of hell are found in the gospels (Matt. 7:19, 8:12, 13:40–50, 22:13, 24:51, 25:30; Luke 16:28; Rev. 14:9–12).
- While hell (sheol) and the lake of fire are not exactly the same, both will end up together. Hell, or sheol, is the holding place of the souls of the wicked dead. At the end of time, both death and hell will be cast into the lake that burns with fire and brimstone (Rev. 20:10, 12–14).

Instructor Notes: Eternity and Beyond

Most of us love pleasant surprise such as a birthday celebration, a baby shower, an anniversary, a graduation, or any number of other celebratory events. It is heartwarming to know that someone loves us enough or cares enough to show a special kind of love and appreciation for us.

That must be, at least in part, what God has in mind for us with regard to eternity. He shares just enough to let us know that eternity with Him will surpass anything we can comprehend or imagine. He tells us what the physical characteristics of the millennial city will look like, and that is absolutely amazing! But He shares precious little about the details of eternity and what it holds for us.

It would be great if the class could read Revelation 21–22. It would be time well spent. We know there will be no more death, pain, or sorrow (Rev. 21:4–5). God, Himself, will wipe all tears from our eyes. Every soul will be blessed. Every human body in the kingdom will be made whole and set free of the boundaries and limitations of mortality (1 Cor. 15:51–58). He exclaims, "Behold, I make all things new!" (Rev. 21:5). Imagine that—all things new! Nothing we knew before will hurt us ever again. His people will live with Him forever.

Eternity and Beyond: Behold—I Make All Things New

- The apostle John saw a new heaven and a new earth coming down from God out of heaven. Behold, the tabernacle of God is with men, and He will dwell with them and they shall be His people (Rev. 21:1–3).
- And God will wipe away every tear from their eyes and there shall be no more death, nor sorrow nor crying. There shall be no more pain for the former things are passed away (Rev. 21:4).
- Heaven will be a phenomenal place of indescribable beauty and majesty. Notice that Jesus only shows John some of the exterior features of the New City, yet that brief description stirs our souls and causes us to long to see Him in all of His glory (Rev. 21–22).
- Gold, pearls, jewels, precious stones, gems, a river of water pure as crystal, no night, no temple, no lamp, no sun. What a place!
- Jesus speaks: "I am the Alpha and the Omega, the beginning and the end. Behold I come quickly and my reward is with me to give every man according as his works shall be. Surely I come Quickly." Even so, Come Lord Jesus! Maranatha!

The Lord closes the book of Revelation with a last call for anyone who is thirsty; anyone who hears is invited to come and drink of the Water of Life freely (Rev. 22:17). Then the Lord sends a warning, an admonition to the teachers of the Word: "Do not add and do not take from His Word" (Rev. 22:18–19). Finally, as we prepare to enter into eternity, Jesus Christ says, "Surely I come quickly Amen. Even so, come Lord Jesus" (Rev. 22:20). Maranatha!

Notes Q&A
Food for Thought

Pre-Test Answer Sheet

This worksheet is for your information only. It will not be graded or corrected except by you. We will review it at the beginning of class and again at the end of the class to compare your growth level. Use it as a Study Guide to help you work through the book of Revelation.

1. The word *rapture* occurs frequently and unmistakably in scripture. **False.** The English word *rapture* does not appear in the Bible, but the Greek word *harpaizo* does appear and is translated as "catching away," "snatching away" or "caught up" (1 Thess. 4:17; 2 Thess. 2:1; 1 Cor. 15:51–58).

2. Believers as well as unbelievers will have to go through the Tribulation. **False.** God said that teaching the truths regarding the Rapture would be a "comfort" to the church (1 Thess. 4:18). He told us to "pray that we would be counted worthy to escape" (Luke 21:34). Why would He tell us to pray to escape what is inevitable? God has never destroyed the righteous with the wicked (Genesis 18:23–26). Jesus's shed blood has made us righteous. When we believed in Him and accepted Him as our Savior, our salvation and redemption were secured. In Psalm 145:17–20, the Lord promised to "preserve" the righteous and destroy the wicked.

3. God's purpose in allowing believers to go through the Tribulation will be to purify the church. False. The blood of Jesus Christ alone purifies God's church. There is no redemption value in the Tribulation (Eph. 1:7).

4. One purpose for the Rapture of the church is to take the saints to heaven where they will receive their reward. **True.** "For the son of Man shall come in the glory of His father with His angels; and then He shall reward every man according to his works" (Matt 16:27); "Behold I come quickly and my reward is with me" (Rev. 22:12).

5. The Holy Spirit will be removed from the earth at the Rapture. **True**/False. The "restraining" power of the Holy Spirit will be taken away at the Rapture and evil will be rampant. However, great multitudes will be saved by the power of the Holy Spirit during the Great Tribulation, but many will be killed for their faith in Jesus Christ (2 Thess. 2:6–8; Rev. 7:9–17).

6. The real purpose of the Great Tribulation is to deal with all unbelievers and punish them for their sins and to deal with God's chosen people, the Jews. **True** (Dan. 9:1–27; Rev. 6:1, 19:1–21; Matt. 24).

7. During the Tribulation, no one will be saved. False. Multitudes (an unknown number) will be saved as a result of the preaching of the gospel by the 144,000 Jewish evangelists (Rev. 7:1–8, 9–17).

8. It is advisable to wait until the Great Tribulation to be saved so God will know how strong and sincere you are. False. If you cannot contend with the devil down here now with the power of the Holy Spirit keeping him in check, how will you deal with him when evil is unleashed and rampant? (Jer. 12:5). "In the day that you hear my voice, harden not your heart" (Heb. 3:7–11). Get saved now while you have a chance!

9. There is evidence in the world today of the mark of the Beast. True (Rev. 13:16–18). Note your evening news! Numbers such as Social Security numbers, ATM/bank account numbers, passwords, PIN numbers, and a host of other numbering systems already allow or prevent you from conducting business. Technologies that allow implanting chips and other identification mechanisms under the skin, in the palm, in teeth, the brain and so on also exist worldwide. This is not to say that the numbers we currently use are the mark of the Beast but simply that these are examples of how this level of control can be achieved during the tribulation period. Cashless society!

10. The Battle of Armageddon is not mentioned in the Bible. False. "And He gathered them together into a place called in the Hebrew tongue, Armageddon" (Rev. 16:16); the Hill or Valley of Megiddo (2 Chron. 35:22; Zech. 12:11).

11. The Battle of Armageddon is the final battle of all time. False. The Battle of Armageddon will precede the Second Coming of Jesus Christ prior to the start of the Millennium. After a thousand years, Satan will be loosed for a little season. He will immediately go about to deceive many. The enemy will be overthrown in the battle of Gog and Magog (Rev. 20:7–9) that will be the final battle.

12. The Rapture and the Second Coming are one and the same. False. At the Rapture, Jesus comes for His church; we will meet Him in the air, at which time He will reward His bride, the church. At His Second Coming, He comes with His church to rule on earth as He promised (Jude 24–25; 1 Thess. 4:13–18).

13. The belief that Jesus will come back to earth and set up an earthly kingdom is symbolic, a figure of speech. False. Absolutely not symbolic! God cannot lie. He said He would return to take His church to His Father's house (John 14:1–3), and we believe exactly what He said! He said that He will set up a righteous kingdom and that the saints will rule with Him (see Isa. 9:6–7; Dan. 2:44–45, 7:13–14; Zech. 14:1–9ff; Acts 15:14–17; Luke 1:32–33).

14. King David will actually rule over a portion of the Lord's millennial kingdom. True. Not only David but also the Lord promised the saints that if we remained faithful, we would reign with Him as heirs and joint heirs of Jesus Christ (Isa. 9:6–7; Acts 15:14–17; Jer. 30:8–9).

15. The earth will be populated during the Millennium, and these people will go up to New Jerusalem to worship the Lord. True. Survivors of the Great Tribulation and resurrected tribulation saints will populate the kingdom of God on earth. They will go up to New Jerusalem to worship and will live in the presence of Jesus for 1,000 years (Isa. 66:23, 66:18; Rev. 21:1–7, 20:4, 20:6).

16. A host of angels will bind Satan for 1,000 years. False (Rev. 20:1–2). One angel with a great chain will bind Satan.

17. New Jerusalem will be the capital city of the millennial kingdom. True (Rev. 21:1–3; Isa. 2:2–3).

18. After the 1,000 years have been completed, no one will ever serve Satan again. False (Rev. 20:7–9). When the thousand years are over, Satan will be loosed from the pit and will immediately go out to deceive the nations once again. Many will follow him and be destroyed.

19. Hell and the lake of fire are the same place. True/False. The terms are often used interchangeably; however, according to Revelation 20:13–14, both death and hell will be cast into the lake of fire. Hell, or sheol, is the holding place for the souls of the wicked dead. Technically, they will end up being the same.

20. One day, the saints will gather around the great white throne. False (Rev. 20:11–15). The wicked dead will be resurrected to stand before God to see if their names are written in the Lamb's Book of Life. Clearly, their names will not be there or they would have risen at the Rapture when the first trumpet sounded and the "dead in Christ" rose first (1 Thess. 4:13–18). The Great White Throne Judgment will be a judgment of the wicked dead.

21. New Jerusalem will come down from heaven to earth. True (Rev. 21:2–3).

22. We will be bored to tears in heaven because we will just sing and pray all day. False. "Know ye not that the saints shall judge the world?" (1 Cor. 6:2). We will participate in the governance of the Lord's kingdom. Matthew 25:21 says that if we are "faithful over a few things He will make us ruler over many." This is prophetic and speaks of a portion of our duties, responsibilities, and rewards given to us in the Lord's millennium kingdom.

23. Just like in church, there will be no eating or drinking in the New City. False. We will participate in the Marriage Supper of the Lamb (Rev. 19:7–9); we will take Holy Communion with Jesus in His father's kingdom (Matt. 26:26–29); citizens of the kingdom will eat from the leaves of the tree on either side of the river and receive healing for their bodies (Rev. 22:2).

24. Does it really matter whether or not you are Pre-Tribulation, Mid-Trib, or Post-Trib? No if you do not believe it matters if the church is scheduled to go through the tribulation or not. Further, if you do not trust that God is truthful and consistent when He said He would not destroy the righteous with the wicked, then it doesn't matter. But if you do believe God's Word, you are definitely Pre-Trib. The fact is, Jesus is definitely coming back, and His church must be ready regardless of where you choose to place the Rapture, the Tribulation, or the Millennium.

25. The saints will be invited to the Supper of the Great God. False. According to Revelation 19:17–21, the birds and fowl of the air will eat the flesh of mighty men, of horses, and of all those who gathered to make war against the coming of our Lord.

26. The saints should be fearful of Revelation because it contains the details of scary things about the end of the world. False. Revelation does indeed contain details about the end of time, but as saints of the Most High, we need to know that we are victorious in the end through Jesus Christ our Lord. Therefore, we have nothing to fear in this magnificent book; rather, it holds victory, praise, and joy in the Holy Spirit! Revelation is the only book in the Bible that promises a blessing to the reader and the hearer as well as to those who keep—believe and hold fast to—the prophecy of the book (Rev. 1:3).

27. Although the church-age saints may not be in the 144,000, we are definitely in that number that no man can number. False. The saints will already have been redeemed by the blood of Jesus Christ, raptured, and in heaven with the Lord. The "number that no man can number" is the fruit of the labors of the 144,000. As they evangelize the world, untold numbers will be saved and converted to Christianity. They are often referred to as the tribulation saints. Most will have to give their lives for accepting Christ during this time of phenomena, suffering, and tribulation. Jesus said in Matthew 24 that there has never been a time like this before and there will never be a time like it again.

28. The church will be at the Battle of Armageddon. True. The church will return with Jesus Christ and the armies of heaven to end the battle. The enemies of Christ will be destroyed with the brightness of His coming. We will have a visual demonstration of 2 Chronicles 20, where we will show up dressed in white, and white horses will be the mode of transportation, but we will "have no need to fight" (Jude 14; Rev. 19:11).

29. Are you saved? Yes_____No

30. Are you sure? Yes_____No

The Seven Churches of Asia Minor Answer Sheets

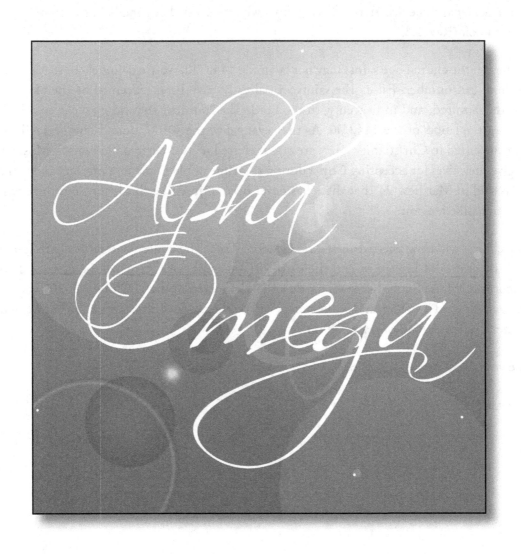

Notes Q&A
Food for Thought

_____

_____

_____

_____

_____

_____

_____

_____

_____

_____

_____

_____

_____

_____

_____

_____

To: The Angel of the Church at Ephesus (Rev. 2:1–7) Church 1
From: He who holds the seven stars in his right hand and walks among the seven golden lampstands

I. **The Acknowledgment:**
 1. I know your works.
 2. Thy patience.
 3. That thou cannot tolerate evil men.
 4. Thou has tested those who claim to be apostles but found them to be liars.
 5. Thou hast persevered.
 6. Thou hast endured hardships, labored for my name, and have not fainted.

II. **The Indictment:**
 1. I have somewhat against you; I will come unto thee quickly.
 2. Forsaken your first love.

III. **The Requirement:**
 1. He who has an ear, let him hear what the Spirit says to the churches.
 2. Repent from where you have fallen and do the things you did at first.

IV. **The Ultimatum:**
 1. Repent and do the things you did at first or …
 2. I will come to you and remove your lampstand from its place.

V. **The Exhortation:**
 1. You do have this, that you hate the doctrine of the Nicolaitans, which I also hate.

VI. **The Blessing/Promise:**
 1. To him that over cometh will I give to eat of the tree of life which is in the midst of the paradise of God.

Notes Q&A
Food for Thought

_____

_____

_____

_____

_____

_____

_____

_____

_____

_____

_____

_____

_____

_____

_____

_____

To: The Angel of the Church at Smyrna (Rev. 2:8–11) Church 2
From: He who is the first and the last, which was dead and is alive

I. **The Acknowledgment:**
1. I know your works.
2. I know thy afflictions.
3. Thy poverty, yet thou art rich.
4. Thy blasphemy of them which say they are Jews but are not.

II. **The Prophecy:**
1. Fear none of those things which thou shalt suffer; the devil shall cast some of you into prison that ye may be tried.
2. Ye shall have tribulation ten days (ye are about to suffer—metaphor for short time).

III. **The Requirement:**
1. Be faithful even unto death and I will give you a Crown of Life.

IV. **The Ultimatum:**
1. He who has an ear let him hear what the Spirit says unto the churches, or …

V. **The Blessing/Promise:**
1. He that overcomes will not be hurt by the second death.

Notes Q&A
Food for Thought

_____

_____

_____

_____

_____

_____

_____

_____

_____

_____

_____

_____

_____

_____

_____

_____

_____

To: The Angel of the Church at Pergamos (Rev. 2:12–17) Church 3
From: He who has the Sharp Sword with two edges

I. **The Acknowledgment:**
   1. I know your works.
   2. That you dwell where Satan's seat is.
   3. Thou has remained true to my name; hast not denied my name even in the times when Antipas my faithful servant was martyred.

II. **The Indictment:**
   1. I have a few things against you; I will come unto thee quickly.
   2. You have them there that hold to the teachings of Balaam, who taught Balak to entice the Israelites to sin.
   3. Taught them to eat things sacrificed to idols.
   4. Taught them to commit fornication.
   5. Also have those who hold to the doctrines of the Nicolaitans, which things I hate.

III. **The Requirement/The Ultimatum:**
   1. Repent or else I will come unto thee quickly … or …
   2. I will fight against them with the sword of my mouth.

IV. **The Exhortation:**
   1. He who has an ear let him hear what the Spirit saith unto the churches.

V. **The Blessing/Promise:**
   1. To him that over cometh will I give to eat of the hidden manna.
   2. I will also give him a white stone with a new name written on it known only to him who receives it.

*N*otes Q&A
*F*ood for Thought

_____

_____

_____

_____

_____

_____

_____

_____

_____

_____

_____

_____

_____

_____

_____

_____

_____

_____

_____

To: The Angel of the Church at Thyatira (Rev. 2:18–29) Church 4
From: The Son of God who has eyes like a flaming fire and feet like fine brass

I. The Acknowledgment:
1. Thy hard works, charity and patience.
2. I know thy service and the last to be more than the first.

II. The Indictment:
1. I have a few things against you.
2. You suffer that woman Jezebel, which calls herself a prophetess, to teach and seduce my servants.
3. To commit fornication and to eat things sacrificed to idols.
4. I gave her space to repent of her fornication and she repented not.

III. The Prophecy:
1. I will cast her into a bed with them that commit adultery with her into great tribulation, except they repent of their deeds.
2. And I will kill her children with death and all the churches will know that I am He who searches the reins and the hearts.
3. I will give every one of you according to your deeds.

IV. The Requirement/Exhortation:
1. He who has an ear, let him hear what the Spirit says to the churches.
2. And to the rest of you that have not known the depths of Satan, I will put no other burden upon you.
3. But that which you have, hold fast until I come.

V. The Blessing/Promise:
1. And he that over cometh and keepeth my words unto the end, to him will I give power over the nations.
2. And he shall rule them with a rod of iron as the vessels of the potter shall they be broken to shivers even as I received of my Father.
3. And I will give him the Morning Star.

Notes Q&A
Food for Thought

_____

_____

_____

_____

_____

_____

_____

_____

_____

_____

_____

_____

_____

_____

_____

_____

To: The Angel of the Church at Sardis (Rev. 3:1–6) Church 5
From: He who has the Seven Spirits of God and the Seven Stars

I. **The Acknowledgment/Indictment:**
1. I know thy works.
2. That thou hast a name that thou livest, but are dead.
3. I have not found your works perfect before God.

II. **The Requirement:**
1. Be watchful!
2. Strengthen those things that remain, that are ready to die.
3. Remember therefore, how you have received and heard, and hold fast.

III. **The Ultimatum:**
1. If therefore thou shalt not watch, I will come upon thee as a thief and thou shalt not know what hour I shall come.

IV. **Additional Acknowledgment:**
1. Thou hast a few names even in Sardis, which have not defiled their garments and they shall walk with me in white: for they are worthy.

V. **The Exhortation:**
1. He that hath an ear let him hear what the Spirit says unto the churches.

VI. **The Blessing/Promise:**
1. He that overcometh, the same shall be clothed in white raiment and I will not blot out his name out of the Book of Life, but will confess his name before my Father and before His angels.

Notes Q&A
Food for Thought

_____

_____

_____

_____

_____

_____

_____

_____

_____

_____

_____

_____

_____

_____

_____

_____

_____

_____

To: The Angel of the Church at Philadelphia (Rev. 3:7–13) Church 6
From: He that is holy, He that is true, He that hath the key of David, He that openeth and no man shutteth, He that shutteth and no man openeth

I. **The Acknowledgment:**
1. I know thy works.
2. Thou hast a little strength and hath kept my word and hath not denied my name.

II. **The Beholdings:**
1. Behold I have set before thee an open door.
2. And no man can shut it.
3. Thou has a little strength.
4. I will make them of the synagogue of Satan which say they are Jews and are not.
5. I will make them to come and worship at thy feet and to know that I have loved thee.
6. Behold I come quickly.

III. **More Acknowledgments:**
1. Because thou hast kept the word of my patience, I also will keep thee from the hour of temptation which shall come upon all the world to try them that dwell upon the earth.

IV. **The Indictment:**
1. None.

V. **The Requirement:**
1. He who has an ear, let him hear what the Spirit says to the churches.

VI. **The Final Exhortation:**
1. Hold fast to that which thou hast that no man take thy crown.

VII. **The Blessing/Promise:**
1. To him that overcometh will I make a pillar in the temple of my God; and he shall go no more out: and I will write upon him the name of my God and the name of the city of my God, which is New Jerusalem, which cometh down out of heaven from my God: and I will write upon him my new name.

Notes Q&A
Food for Thought

_____

_____

_____

_____

_____

_____

_____

_____

_____

_____

_____

_____

_____

_____

_____

_____

_____

_____

_____

To: the Angel of the Church at Laodicea (Rev. 3:14–22) Church 7
From: The Amen, the faithful and the true witness, the beginning of the creation

I. **The Acknowledgment**
    1. Thy works.

II. **The Indictment:**
    1. That thou are neither hot nor cold.
    2. I would that thou were cold or hot.
    3. So then because thou are lukewarm, I will spue thee out of my mouth.
    4. Because thou saith, I am rich and increased with goods and have need of nothing and knowest not that thou are wretched and miserable and poor and blind and naked.

III. **The Requirement/The Ultimatum:**
    1. I counsel thee to buy of me, gold tried in the fire, that thou mayest be rich;
    2. and white raiment that thou mayest be clothed and that the shame of thy nakedness do not appear;
    3. and anoint thine eyes with eye-salve that thou mayest see.
    4. As many as I love, I rebuke and chasten.

IV. **The Exhortation:**
    1. Be zealous therefore and repent.

V. **The Blessing/Promise:**
    1. Behold I stand at the door and knock: If any man hears my voice and open the door, I will come in to him and will sup with him and he with me. To him that overcometh will I grant to sit with me in my throne, even as I also overcame and am set down with my Father. He that hath an ear, let him hear what the Spirit saith to the churches.

Notes Q&A
Food for Thought

_____

_____

_____

_____

_____

_____

_____

_____

_____

_____

_____

_____

_____

_____

_____

_____

_____

_____

_____

_____

References, Resources and Additional Reading

Hitchcock, Mark. *101 Answers to Questions about the Book of Revelation*. Eugene, OR: Harvest House Publishers, 2012.

Jeremiah, David. *Agents of the Apocalypse*. San Diego: Turning Point for God, 2014.

Jeremiah, David with C. C. Carlson. *Escape the Coming Night*. Nashville: Thomas Nelson, 1997.

Jeremiah, David. *Prophetic Turning Points*. San Diego: Turning Point for God, 2001.

Jeremiah, David. *The Handwriting on the Wall*. San Diego: Turning Point for God, 2007.

LaHaye, Tim. *A Quick Look at the Rapture and the Second Coming*. Eugene, OR: Harvest House Publishers, 2013.

LaHaye, Tim and Thomas Ice. Eugene, OR: Harvest House Publishers, 2002.

MacArthur, John. "A Jet Tour Through the Book of Revelation." http://www.gty.org/Broadcast/ transcripts/ (accessed July 27, 2001).

MacArthur, John. "Back to the Future Part I."

http://www.gty.org/Broadcast/transcripts/66-1.htm (accessed July 27, 2001).

MacArthur, John. "Back to the Future Part II."

http://www.gty.org/Broadcast/transcripts/66-2.htm (accessed July 27, 2001).

MacArthur, John. "The Certainty of the Second Coming."

http://www.gty.org/Broadcast/transcripts/66-3.htm (accessed July 27, 2001).

Perkins, Donald. *Bible Prophecy: God's Order of Events*. Lemon Grove, CA: According to Prophecy Ministries, 2002.

Reagan, David R. *Christ in Prophecy A Study Guide*. McKinney, TX: Lamb & Lion Ministries, 2006.

Smith, Chuck with David Wimbish. *The Last Days, The Middle East and The Book of Revelation*. Grand Rapids, MI: Chosen Books, a division of Baker House Company, 1992.

Swaggart, Jimmy. *A Study in Bible Prophecy: A Scriptural Approach to Eschatology*. Baton Rouge, LA: Jimmy Swaggart Ministries, 1986.

Unger, Merrill F., revised by Gary N. Larson. *The New Unger's Bible Handbook*. Chicago: Moody Press, 1998.

Contact Information

Evangelist Mary L. Page MAABS, MPA, BSBM
Speaker Requests—Series—Classes—Workshops—Seminars—Special Events

New Season Ministries of San Diego Inc.
A Division of Henry Page Ministries Inc.
P.O. Box 212378
Chula Vista, CA 91914

Mobile (619) 306–3706 Fax: (619) 934–6063
Email: marylpage@yahoo.com
Follow us on FaceBook Website Under Construction

Printed in the United States
By Bookmasters